SEXING THE TEXT

SEXING THE TEXT

*The Rhetoric of Sexual Difference in
British Literature, 1700–1750*

Todd C. Parker

STATE UNIVERSITY OF NEW YORK PRESS

Published by
State University of New York Press
© 2000 State University of New Y ork
All rights reserved
Printed in the United States of America

For information, address the State University of New York Press,
State University Plaza, Albany, NY 12246

Marketing by Patrick Durocher • Production by Bernadine Dawes

Library of Congress Cataloging-in-Publication Data

Parker, Todd C., 1965–
    Sexing the text : the rhetoric of sexual difference in British literature, 1700–1750 / Todd
C. Parker.
        p.   cm.
    Includes bibliographical references (p.) and index.
    ISBN 0-7914-4485-6 (hc : alk. paper)—ISBN 0-7914-4486-4 (pb : alk. paper)
    1. English literature—18th century—History and criticism. 2. Sex differences
(Psychology) in literature. 3. English language—18th century—Rhetoric. 4. Sex
differences in literature. 5. Body, Human, in literature. 6. Masculinity in literature. 7.
Femininity in literature. 8. Sex role in literature. 9. Sex in literature. I. Title.

PR448.S45 P37 2000
820.9'3538'0905—dc21
                                                                                    99-056707

        1   2   3   4   5   6   7   8   9   10

To James L. and Connie Capers Thorson
with love and gratitude

Contents

Acknowledgments

> There are certain common Privileges of a Writer, the
> Benefit whereof, I hope, there will be no Reason to doubt;
> Particularly, that where I am not understood, it shall be
> concluded, that something very useful and profound is
> coucht beneath, And again, that whatever word or Sentence
> is Printed in a different Character, shall be judged to contain
> something extraordinary either of *Wit* or *Sublime*.
> —Preface to *A Tale of a Tub*

Swift's words ring encouragingly in my ears as this project nears completion. Many people have contributed to what is, I hope, "very useful and profound" in this work, and my thanks are heartfelt. First, to Fredric V. Bogel, Laura Brown, and Neil Saccamano, who saw this project from its inception to its defense as a dissertation at Cornell University. Krystyna Mazur, Francesca Sawaya, Cathy Tufariello, Teresa Feroli, and Susan Gilmore all read and suffered patiently through multiple drafts of various chapters; Susan in particular was an integral part of the intellectual process that makes research and writing rewarding. Paul Sawyer and Wendy Jones were the best of intellectual companions. Kevin Cope of Louisiana State University, Baton Rouge, proved to be an exemplary editor, and his comments on an early stage of the *Onania* chapter were invaluable. Clement Hawes of Southern Illinois University has been a good friend both to me and to my manuscript; he especially has my thanks for his careful response to chapter 4.

I wish to thank my colleague at DePaul University, Bill Fahrenbach, for being consistently supportive. Bill has been a loyal friend and an exacting reader: I envy him his close-reading skills, and I extend my thanks for his time, insight, and abundant goodwill.

I am also grateful to the readers who reviewed my work for the State University of New York Press; I profited considerably from their criticism and encouragement. James Peltz has shepherded the manuscript through each stage of production with wit and affability and has proved that most rare of academic phenomena, a prompt correspondent.

My thanks to the Graduate School of Cornell University for an A. D. White Fellowship, to the Jacob K. Javits Fellowship program, and to the Mellon Foundation. DePaul University gave me much-needed research support in the form of grants from the College of Liberal Arts and Sciences Summer Research Program. Thanks also to John Hopper, editor-in-chief at AMS Press, for permission to reprint the *Onania* chapter.

I have dedicated this book to Jim and Connie Thorson as meager repayment for the effort and affection they have invested in me. If I can pinpoint a time when my career began to take shape, it was surely that moment in his survey of English literature when Jim first brought Jonathan Swift so convincingly to life for a room full of unsuspecting first-year undergraduates.

I owe my deepest debt of gratitude, though, to my parents, Earl and Beverly Parker, and to my brother, Eric. Their enthusiasm and unhesitating generosity underwrite every felicitous phrase and insight of which this project can boast.

Introduction: Sexuality and the "Natural" Subject of the Early Eighteenth Century

The opposition between "male" and "female" is one that pervades English literature of the earlier eighteenth century and that this work takes not as a starting point, but rather as the culmination of a difficult negotiation between competing ideologies of the gendered subject. This conflict is the result of a reformulation of male sexuality that takes place around the time of the Restoration and that is largely complete by the middle of the century. For eighteenth-century Britain, male sexuality, instead of signaling a masculine identity sensitive to its class and immediate environment, becomes increasingly the privileged site of an emerging heterosexual hierarchy defining "male" as that which corresponds to "female" as a limit. This limiting effect, I argue, establishes the modern period as such, since it is only by instating a self-limiting logic of hetero-sexual duality that the political conventions of modern subjectivity become possible. Nancy Armstrong acknowledges the power of this emergent hierarchy when she writes,

> So basic are the terms "male and "female" to the semiotics of modern life that no one can use them without to some

1

degree performing the very reifying gesture whose operations we would like to understand and whose power we want to historicize. Whenever we cast our political lot in the dyadic formation of gender, we place ourselves in a classic double bind, which confines us to alternatives that are not really alternatives at all. That is to say, any political position founded primarily on sexual identity ultimately confirms the limited choices offered by such a dyadic model. Once one thinks within such a structure, sexual relationships appear as the model for all power relationships.[1]

The force of Armstrong's critique derives partly from her awareness that "male" and "female" are the terms in which we think, whether we wish to or not, and in which our culture invests much of its naturalizing literary capital. If, as a consequence, Armstrong appears to limit the political potential of modern sexual identity, it is because the system of sexual identity she examines is determined primarily by the opposition her work attempts to displace. This is not to say that the male/female binarism always works identically in eighteenth-century texts. As the following chapters make evident, this binarism constantly shifts political ground as it tries to prioritize differing historical representations of gender and of bodies made explicitly sexual as part of a greater political strategy for controlling individual identity and communal association. Nor do I claim that the male/female binarism is an opposition of equal terms, since as we will see, the power of this binarism often depends upon the historical and rhetorical subordination of female to male, especially in the representation of same-sex relationships. But the possibility of a stable categorical opposition between male and female bodies, personalities, and character traits proves irresistible to the authors I examine, even when the attempt to stabilize that opposition requires significant categorical violence in its own right.

By purveying "natural" sexual difference as the meaning of

earlier eighteenth-century sexuality, the works I discuss restrict allowable forms of personal identity in a period of British history when sexual identity becomes the focal point of political and economic pressure. Heterosexual difference as a universal category, the very ahistoricity of which defines it as "natural," insures the coordination of male and female bodies, productive and unproductive practices, natural and unnatural sexual activities, and most important of all, proper and perverse political communities. As a result, vital social hierarchies of both public and private life are, in the language of sexual difference that becomes prevalent in eighteenth-century British life, guaranteed by innate sexual orientation. Many of the constituent terms for what I will call the rhetoric of sexual difference are for the first time argued out textually in ways we as modern individuals recognize because we have inherited and internalized these arguments as natural and therefore unquestionable. The earlier eighteenth century locates a political origin for these terms because it is, as Laura Brown writes, "the first major age of English imperialism, the age of the powerful consolidation of a consensus of economic expansion, and of an energetic, wide-ranging, but incomplete ideological hegemony"[2] that includes the hegemony of "natural" heterosexuality in the field of gender relations and in the reproduction of specific political identities.

In the following essays, I will attempt to situate my own understanding of the heterosexual binarism male/female by questioning the stability of this central opposition in the history of eighteenth-century English sexuality and by displacing the oppositional hierarchy underwriting heterosexuality. My work in an important sense tries to extend this displacement by examining exemplary moments in the literary history of sexual difference. From 1700 on, I contend, competing ideologies of sexuality and sexual identity begin to give way to an overriding construct of natural heterosexuality that in its turn depends on men and women who are rhetorically constituted as different from each other. We move, in other words, from a plurality of sexual practices legitimated by class and social rank to a dominant representation of sexuality in which male and female bodies naturally and inevitably invoke each other. This is not to argue that pre-Restoration sexuality, and particularly male sexual identity, is somehow open-ended or fluid in a utopian sense; it is instead to recognize how the discursive constraints that constitute such sexuality change historically. By the time we reach John Cleland's novels of the late 1740s and early 1750s, sexual difference has become the eminent characteristic of a primarily sexual subjectivity extending *to* men and women and invoking subjects *as* "men" and "women" in the first place. This move is not an easy one, and the resulting discourse remains riven by internal contradictions and omissions that the process of heterosexual hegemonization leaves in its wake. In the texts I will consider, gender as a meaningful category of literary representation often emerges only after a complicated series of rhetorical maneuvers whereby the author posits some heterosexual state for his or her characters that the text must then attempt to enact as if heterosexuality were culturally unmotivated. The text's task is to reproduce this "natural" sexuality as simply a series of illustrations of itself, so that the typical markers for "natural" sexuality become sexually differentiated male and female bodies. Reading sexuality off the ideal body is, in other words, simply a confirmation of the natural identity inhering in that body as a necessary correlative of sexual difference. But for the ruse of natural sexuality to succeed, reading—a differentiating act in itself—must appear to be only a form of transparent observation. These essays try to make the artifice of this transparency visible.

As Thomas Laqueur has pointed out, the history of sexual difference as a vehicle for gendered identity changes significantly from the beginning of the eighteenth century to its close. Laqueur argues that pre-Enlightenment sexuality organized itself according to an ancient and Galenic model in which men and women shared the same biological morphisms and differed only in their relative degrees of "perfection":

> Sometime in the eighteenth century, sex as we know it was invented. The reproductive organs went from being paradigmatic sites for displaying hierarchy, resonant throughout the cosmos, to being the foundation of incommensurable difference: "women owe their manner of being to their organs of generation, and especially to the uterus," as one eighteenth-century physician put it. Here was not only an explicit repudiation of the old isomorphisms but also, and more important, a rejection of the ideal that nuanced differences between organs, fluids, and physiological processes mirrored a transcendental order of perfection.[3]

This transition from an isomorphic model of sexual difference as degree to a more "modern" concept of sexual difference as specification meant that the older authorities on human sexuality became progressively obsolete:

> Aristotle and Galen were simply mistaken in holding that female organs are a lesser form of the male's and by implication that woman is a lesser man. A woman is a woman, proclaimed the "moral anthropologist" Moreau in one of the many new efforts to derive culture from the body, everywhere and in all things, moral and physical, not just in one set of organs. (149)

"Woman," in Moreau's model, no longer shares in any encompassing human sexuality. She instead becomes a new species recognizable as such by her difference from man.

Shifting eighteenth-century paradigms were, according to Laqueur, less the result of objectifiable scientific knowledge than of the ideological pressures that changing eighteenth-century British culture placed on available theories of subjectivity:

> The context for the articulation of two incommensurable sexes was, however, neither a theory of knowledge nor advances in scientific knowledge. The context was politics. There were endless new struggles for power and position in the enormously enlarged public sphere of the eighteenth and particularly the postrevolutionary nineteenth centuries: between and among men and women; between and among feminists and anti-feminists. When, for many reasons, a preexisting transcendental order or time-immemorial custom became a less and less plausible justification for social relations, the battleground of gender roles shifted to nature, to biological sex. (152)

By conflating contingent political articulations of sexual difference with the category of "nature," eighteenth-century ideologues went a long way toward establishing heterosexual identity as an essential consequence of "the new epistemological status of nature as the bedrock of distinctions" (153). There was, as Laqueur argues, no way to make the epistemological foundation for what would become heterosexual difference a "natural" construct other than to claim "naturalness" as the hallmark of such difference, since

> the nature of sexual difference is not susceptible to empirical testing. It is logically independent of biological facts because already embedded in the language of science, at least when applied to any culturally resonant construal of sexual difference, is the language of gender. (153)

Gender, the cultural intersection of discourse with the body, thus underlies the inevitability of heterosexual difference even as that difference promulgates itself as the "precultural" substrate of human experience.

We can see the changing nature of the constraints on sexuality as a category of identity more clearly if we compare differing interpretations of the same sexual activity. During that dramatically transformative period toward the end of the Restoration when gender roles were beginning to consolidate around the figure of the "natural" man or woman, what had once been viewed as the excessive but comprehensible sexual activity of the Restoration rake, whose abundant sexual attentions could be spent at will on women, boys, or both, became instead a perverse and inexplicable sexual tendency that defined not the libertine, but the sodomite. Randolph Trumbach traces the course of this figure through several analytical essays and finds that "In this world [of aristocratic libertines] the love of boys certainly did not exclude the love of women; but the love of boys was seen as the most extreme act of sexual libertinism"[4] to which the privilege of rank could aspire. Aristocratic male libertines certainly enjoyed sexual freedoms specific to their social position, but as Trumbach records, the aristocratic libertine was himself a public spectacle that displayed male sexuality abroad as a publicly consumed and contained phenomenon. As spectacle, the libertine's sexuality was thus available to all classes and sexes in British life. We find, for instance, that it is in the world of libertine sexual display that

> the twenty-four-year-old Sir Charles Sedley stood naked on the balcony of an inn and in full daylight, "showed his nakedness," "acting all the postures of lust and buggery that could be imagined," abused the Scriptures, and preached that he had such a powder to sell, "as should make all the cunts in town run after him." He was punished by the magistrate.[5]

By "acting all the postures of lust and buggery that could be imagined," Sedley aligns his sexual desire with both boys and women in an exemplary act of civic libertinage, since "imagining" lust and buggery means locating those acts in a field of sexual possibilities that Sedley and his appalled audience share.[6] But by recognizably acting out such postures alone, Sedley also reveals how sexuality could still be detached from the heterosexual matrix of male/female and how these sexual postures of "lust and buggery" could recuperate Sedley's sexuality as part of his more "natural" sinfulness. While same-sex sodomy figures here primarily as a crime against Scripture, it is at least implicitly an extension of the aristocratic male body's inborn predisposition toward sinful sexual excess, a predisposition that in its turn defines the spectacle of the libertine's unconventional sexuality.

Libertines, Trumbach contends, were not the objects of social scorn for their sexual excesses precisely because those excesses signified a superior form of masculinity that transcended the limitations of quotidian society.[7] That is, from the beginning of the seventeenth century on, Sedley's sort of rakish display was a sign of true libertine identity, and his aggressive appetite made whatever sodomizing or effeminizing sexual excess in which he chose to engage an expression of his masculine desires. Reading along with Alan Bray, Trumbach stresses the doubled meanings sodomy and effeminacy took on as the libertine moved through seventeenth-century society:

> However defined, sodomy was often seen as the final step of a sexual sinner after rape, adultery, and incest. Sodomites were classed also as part of an infernal trio of "sorcerers, sodomites, and heretics," and were not viewed, therefore, as exclusively sexual persons. Sodomy was only one, if the gravest, of the sexual disorders to break out when marriage (the bulwark against debauchery) was ignored. Bray also

points out that the word "effeminacy" was in the early seventeenth century similarly protean, sometimes used to describe cross-dressing boys but also to describe men who had become weakened through excessive sexual contact with women.[8]

Both "sodomy" and "effeminacy," then, pertain in the context of the seventeenth century to male bodies that exceed the proper limits set for sexual desires. As a consequence, seventeenth-century use of the term "effeminacy" applied principally to an improper desire for the female body and only later came to designate a sexual role the rakish male aristocrat could be seen as filling himself. If "sodomy" in this period was an ambiguous term signifying anyone's sinful potential, "effeminacy," too, had multiple applications to the rakish male body. But having these desires did not mean that the male subject exchanged a "natural" sexual identity for another and "perverse" identity when engaged in sodomitical or effeminizing sexual contact. Indeed, for men of station, transgressive sexual intercourse reaffirmed masculinity and gestured toward its social potential if it could only be contained by marriage and its energies channeled into the dynamo of reproduction. Sexual excess was the effect of sin, and it was sin that determined the contours of the libertine's masculinity. "Effeminacy" and "sodomy" thus paradoxically become signs of superior masculinity in the seventeenth century, and it is only by replacing the libertine's omnivorous male sexuality with a masculinity that has one, and only one, natural correspondent that same-sex sodomy becomes the exemplary crime against nature.

This transition from comprehensible forms of male sodomy to the "perverse" and alienating practices that bear the burden of so much of today's sexual anxiety comes about largely as a result of the change in definition of male sexuality. "Sodomy," both in the early eighteenth century and today, strongly implies some form of anal penetration, but at the same time, the term also resonates with a whole range of sexual practices seen as undermining faith and good government. So G. S. Rousseau argues in an influential essay on the history of homosexuality and sodomy in the eighteenth century that sodomy is only one of a range of homosexual activities from active anal penetration to a more homoerotic sociability.[9] "Sodomy" by this reading becomes neither constitutive of nor inseparably associated with homosexuality in early-eighteenth-century British culture. Rousseau recognizes that for much of the period, "sodomy" acted less to categorize individuals than it did to stigmatize their activities:

> Circa 1700 the *word* "sodomy" denoted a large class of sinners; unlike the *category* sodomy (Foucault's "la sodomie"), it poses fewer problems for interpretation than does the larger class of homosexuality. (136)

But as Cameron McFarlane observes,

> while *buggery* and *sodomy*, especially in religious and legal texts, could and did denote "a confused category" of acts, in many other sources we find increasing evidence of a more narrow and specific usage, a usage in which these words refer first and foremost to sexual contact between two males; likewise *sodomite* comes to refer specifically to a man who engages in a sexual act with another man. (3)

Even though "sodomy" remains a term ambiguously applied both to act and to perpetrator, Rousseau can write that sodomites themselves increasingly had both a lexical and a political prominence in the eighteenth-century landscape. "The homosexual sodomite was a penetrator of males, unlike the larger class of sodomites, who may have committed any number of sexual and nonsexual 'crimes'" (136). The important idea here is that male-male penetration functions as a special case for a larger class of offenses constellated more or less loosely around unauthorized sexual contact, but as H. Montgomery Hyde has written, the evolution of the term "buggery" through the seventeenth century reflects a specific (and specifically political) association with sin and offenses against God, rather than with any specifically biological impetus:

> *Bougre* derived from the Latin *Bulgaris* meaning native of Bulgaria, where the Manichean and Albigensian heresies were known to flourish. The term Bulgar or *Boulgre*, contracted to *bougre*, was gradually applied to all heretics, and from being an abusive term for heresy in general *bougrerie* (buggery) became the common appellation for the supposed sexual habits of heretics and usurers. No doubt some of the Albigensians were homosexuals, as also were the Knights Templars, who were suppressed by the Inquisition, many of the Knights confessing to their practices in the torture chambers of the Holy Office. But by and large the charge of homosexuality seems to have been part of the general "smear" campaign employed by the Inquisition against its enemies. In England, although the word "buggery" was no doubt previously used for some time in the vernacular, it did not become an accepted legal term until made the subject of statue in the reign of Henry VIII.[10]

Human nature, and in particular the nature of male sexuality is throughout this period much more a function of class and inherent sinfulness than it is of any bodily impulse as such. Ed Cohen has written that prior to the pathologization of homosexuality in the later nineteenth century, sexual practices between men were almost universally understood as "sodomy"—a category deriving from canon law that referred exclusively to a particular kind of sexual act whether "committed with mankind or beast." Since sodomy was never conceived of as the antithesis of any normative sexual standard, it was perceived to be a ubiquitous, nonprocreative possibility resulting from the inherent sinfulness of human nature.[11]

Cohen quotes the early-seventeenth-century English jurist Sir Edward Coke's *Third Part of the Institutes of the Laws of England*, which redefines sodomy as "buggery" (to give the unnameable moral crime a legal correspondent):

Buggery is a detestable, and abominable sin, amongst Christians not to be named, commited by carnal knowledge against the ordinance of the creator, and order of nature, by mankind with mankind, or with brute beast, or by womankind with brute beast. (175)

Coke defines sodomy itself as a highly ambiguous physical act: "So as there must be *penetratio,* that is *res in re* [the thing in the thing], either with mankind or with beast, but the least penetration maketh it carnall knowledge" (176). To transform this extremely indeterminate interpretation, which could apply to oral, manual, anal, and other types of sexual contact between both sexes and (theoretically) unlimited numbers of species, into the nineteenth century's specific injunction against male-male contact required shifting the weight of sexual significance from acts to bodies. Cohen describes how the historical permutations of British sodomy laws eventually relocated the "natural" or "unnatural" aspects of sexuality in the way male bodies related to their surroundings:

> [W]hereas "sodomy" had enjoined a particular sexual act
> that was to some extent independent of the sex of the ac-
> tors, "acts of gross indecency" were entirely unspecified in
> themselves and only derived their "indecency" from their
> appearance in the context of a relationship between two
> men. (191)

This 1885 statute went a long way toward legitimating popular
conceptions of "natural" heterosexuality (as contrasted with the
"unnatural" character of sodomitical intercourse) that paralleled
the emergence of separate sexual identities for men and women
that had been coalescing in English culture for over two hundred
years. Trumbach, for instance, points out that English popular literature of the early 1700s was beginning to identify the effeminate
man as a new kind of woman:

> The material from 1709 makes it even clearer that contem-
> poraries were beginning to see a kind of sodomite different
> from the men who frigged and sodomized boys and ad-
> vised them to try lewd women. The new sodomites met as
> clubs in taverns, and they called themselves (according to
> Ned Ward) *mollies*. It is a word probably related to *molly*,
> which meant a female prostitute. . . . It makes clear that the
> sodomite viewed himself, and was seen by others, no longer
> as a rake but as a species of outcast woman.[12]

If the same sodomitical activity that once registered an excessively
masculine sexual desire now turns one into a woman, then both
male and female sexual identities have been reorganized by changing articulations of sodomy. Cohen affirms this reorganization of
gendered subjectivity around sodomy as a newly "unnatural" practice when he quotes a London pamphlet from the 1730s entitled

Plain Reasons for the Growth of Sodomy in England. For the pamphleteer, sodomy is, as Cohen notes, "an extreme form of social dissolution predicated on the negation of the 'manly' ideal," since as the pamphleteer argues, "anything of *Manliness* [is] diametrically opposed to such unnatural Practices."[13]

The best example of this shift from the "sinful" to the "manly" is the early-eighteenth-century response to the case of Mervyn, earl of Castlehaven, who was tried and executed for sodomy and rape in 1631.[14] Castlehaven's case was a turning point both in the history of English sodomy laws and in England's changing sexual consciousness because his trial marked the first successful prosecution for adult homosexuality in Britain since sodomy had been made a felony in 1533.[15] A Catholic, Castlehaven was prosecuted for a variety of crimes: He and his servants Lawrence Fitzpatrick, Henry Skipwith, and Giles Broadway raped Castlehaven's wife, Lady Anne Stanley, and his twelve-year-old daughter-in-law, Elizabeth Audley; Castlehaven played voyeur as Skipwith, acting on Castlehaven's directions, "used oil to enter" Elizabeth;[16] most importantly, Castlehaven used Broadway's body "'as the body of a woman, but never pierced it, only emitted between the thighs'" while Broadway raped Lady Castlehaven.[17] Castlehaven was eventually arrested after his son Audley complained to Charles I about the mistreatment he, as Castlehaven's heir, was receiving at the hands of his father. Audley was particularly offended that Castlehaven wanted Skipwith to father an heir on Elizabeth. On November 1, 1630, Audley wrote to Castlehaven to chide him for his unfatherly conduct and to report that Audley had appealed to "the King's Majesty" for retribution. As Hyde records, Audley particularly complained that because of Castlehaven's actions, "his father's 'own dear branches hang down their heads to see the sap and livelihood conferred upon another,' namely Henry Skipwith."[18] Castlehaven was eventually arrested and tried, and after a long wrangle with the anti-Catholic attorney general Sir Robert Heath over whether or not the statute of Henry VIII applied to sexual acts in which penetration did not take place, Castlehaven was convicted and executed. In "The Tryal and Condemnation of Mervin, Lord Audley of Castlehaven at Westminster. April the 5th 1631," an account of the Castlehaven proceedings that first appeared in 1699, Heath is reported to have argued:

> As to this Indictment there is no other Question, but whether it be *Crimen Sodomiticum penetratione*, whether he penetrated the Body, or not; to which I answer, the Fifth of *Elizabeth*, sets it down in general Terms, and *ubi Lex non distinguis, ibi non distinguendum* [where the law does not distinguish, there let no distinction be made]; and I know you will be cautious how you give the least Mittigation to such abominable Sins; for when once a Man indulges his Lust, and Prevaricates with his Religion, as my Lord *Audley* has done, by being a Protestant in the Morning, and a Papist in the Afternoon, no wonder if he commits the most abominable Impieties; for when Men forsake their God, 'tis no wonder he leaves them to themselves.[19]

It is difficult to tell from Heath's statement whether Castlehaven is being tried more as a sodomite or as a Catholic; indeed the two terms are inseparable in Heath's arguments. While Castlehaven's sexual practices were central to his trial and conviction, Castlehaven was arraigned less for an inexcusable offense that was *only* sexual and more for offenses against his rank as an aristocrat and progenitor of a bloodline, as well as for being a Catholic in a Protestant court. Lawrence Stone argues that Charles I let Castlehaven's conviction stand in an attempt to improve the king's position with an ever more powerful Puritan class:

It looked as if the aristocracy had reason to think themselves immune from both the dictates of conventional morality and the penalties of the law. Charles did something in 1630 [1631] to restore confidence in royal justice by declining to interfere with his peers in the death-sentence imposed by his peers on the Earl of Castlehaven for a series of outrageous sexual offenses, but by now the damage had been done. Throughout the whole of this period archidiaconal courts and town magistrates had been treating the sexual pecca-dilloes of the lower orders with extreme severity, and the discrepancy between the generally enforced moral code and the license of the Court became an established part of pub-lic belief. Impinging upon the puritan conscience, this was a powerful factor in undermining the moral authority of both the peerage and the Court.[20]

As an unpopular Catholic and an aristocrat flaunting the conven-tional morals of his time, Castlehaven was the perfect target for a conservative aristocratic attempt to retrench the flagging "moral authority" of the aristocratic class, but the justification for choosing Castlehaven as victim or scapegoat rests firmly in the seventeenth-century belief that he had indulged his base and sinful nature and that, consequently, God had abandoned him to the fate of all unre-pentant sinners. Sodomy is not, ultimately, the only reason for Castlehaven's execution or for the execution of his servants. B. R. Burg writes that for Castlehaven and his men, "it was the aggre-gate of their social behavior rather than a specific crime that earned them a death sentence. Their trespass over sacred class boundaries only amplified their sexual transgressions."[21] The rationale, how-ever, for Castlehaven's capital sentence is the seventeenth-century logic that makes Castlehaven's sin and his sexuality coextensive. If, in other words, Castlehaven caused a scandal, it was because he had, as Heath maintains, "indulged his Lust, and Prevaricated with his Religion," and for the attorney general, there is no difference in degree or kind between Castlehaven's offenses. The logic of sin Heath voices during Castlehaven's trial requires that Castlehaven die because, as Heath "grieves" to utter, "Justice is the way to cut off all Wickedness," and Castlehaven's "Mortification" must be as "remarkable" as his offences.[22]

Perhaps most noteworthy of the 1699 account is the anonymous preface that introduces Castlehaven to an early-eighteenth-century public. The prefacer begins by "deploring" that England has become a place where "*Wickedness should ascend to such a height, as equals, if not exceeds, all the Barbarous Regions of the Earth*" (A2).[23] The prefacer looks back on a period of English history when

> *gross enormities in this Island, like* Batts *and* Owls *were obscur'd by Night and Darkness, and those that committed them were asham'd to own their Crimes, or suffer their Examples to infect the open Air. They were contented to go to Hell alone, without Usurping the Office of* Belzebub, *or loading their Souls with the Guilt of* Tempting *their incautious Brethren; but now the most* Scandalous, Inhuman, Unnatural, and Beastly Offences, *stalk abroad at Noon day, and he thinks himself a Puny in Wickedness and* scarce worth the Damning, *that can't boast of numbers of Souls that he has lead to Destruction.* (Preface, 2–3)

The prefacer names "Ravishing Women" among these offenses, but the crime that receives most of his attention is "*the* Devillish and Unnatural Sin of Buggery," which "*sinks a Man below the Basest Epithet, is so* Foul *it admits of no Aggravation, and cannot be express'd in its Horror, but by the* Doleful Shrikes and Groans of the Damned" (Preface, 4). The prefacer's ostensible motive for publishing the transcript of Castlehaven's trial is a sense of public duty:

I thought I could not more oblige the Publick, than (having this Tryal lying by me in an Old Manuscript which was never yet Printed,) to Publish it at this Juncture, that by Reading the Sin, so Tragically Delineated in its Horrid Shape, and ugly Visage, by the Grave and Learned Sages of the Law, and in the Death of a Noble Peer, other Men might be terrify'd, and scar'd from those Sins that are attended with nothing but Infamy and Death in this World, and Eternal Damnation in the next. (Preface, 4–5)

To this point, the prefacer's comments simply reiterate the seventeenth-century position defining unconventional sexuality as sin. But as the preface concludes, the prefacer aims his address at the men he hopes to scare into piety, and as the preface's audience changes, so does the prefacer's tone. The prefacer entreats sodomites to

See your Faces . . . on the Pillory, *and the* Brink of Hell, *and if that will neither shame nor fright you; let me beg the favour of you to leave the Kingdom, for that will be the best Office you ever did, or can do for* England, *and the Obligation shall be gratefully acknowledg'd by* Gentlemen, (If it ben't a Shame to Stile you so; Your Humble Servant, The *Prefacer.* [sic] (Preface, 6–7)

Whereas Heath adopts a grieving tone appropriate to the serious nature of Castlehaven's "sin" and calls upon Castlehaven to "think upon the Turpitude of your Offences, with an unfeigned Sorrow, and a Sincere Repentance" (25), the prefacer's closing remarks deride his putative audience even as he claims to make it possible for that audience to repent. Heath's grave and courtly exhortation is certainly appropriate to the king's court, but it also at least implicitly acknowledges that when a man, regardless of who he is, once "indulges his Lust, and Prevaricates with his Religion," that man realizes a universal sinful potential that all postlapsarian men share.

The tone of the prefacer's address, on the other hand, implies that there is something distinctly impolite and unmanly about his sodomitical addressees, since it is a shame to style them "gentlemen," and that these same sodomites are ultimately expendable both as men and as Englishmen. The prefacer's derisive tone excludes such men from the realm of redeemable sinners and relocates them in the category of the inherently perverse. Part of the prefacer's contempt stems from the possibility that his sodomitical audience has ceased to believe in the system of sin and punishment that still motivates the prefacer himself. He angrily asks his hypothetical listeners "Whether they can the better indure Eternal Torment, because they don't believe them? *Or*, whether they can extinguish the Flames of Hell, by going merily and Laughing thither?" (Preface, 6). Unlike Heath's consistent discourse of sin, the prefacer's text is caught in the interstice between a discourse of human nature as sin and a discourse of sexuality and behavior that no longer strictly conforms to religious conventions defining the fallen essence or character of man.

The ideology of masculinity thus begins to change significantly in the early 1700s. If the essential nature of seventeenth-century sexuality, particularly male sexuality, is its "sinfulness," by the middle of the eighteenth century that essential nature has become one of biological urges and conspicuously noncultural sexual desires. These two models for male sexuality locating male identity in humanity's sinfulness or in its biology do not allow for a simple narrative of succession, where seventeenth-century notions of sexuality as part of man's sinful inheritance give way to the new eighteenth-century biologism of two complementary sexes. Instead, the two models compete with each other for ideological primacy during this period, and it is only as part of the long ideological transformation these texts bear witness to that heterosexual difference gains the hegemonic high ground. Trumbach notes that "The libertine was, in the eighteenth century, a dying breed," primarily because conceptions of gender in the first half of the century no longer allow the aggressively sexual man to remain unaffected by the gender of his sexual partner.[24] Rather than being simply the recipient of a man's sexual attentions as had been the predominant interpretation of male sexuality in the seventeenth century, a man's sexual partners now became the source of a contaminating and very modern gender slippage in which the type of one's sexual partner in its turn typified one's self. Trumbach identifies four classes of adult eighteenth-century men who could be defined by the type of their sexual partners: (1) men attracted to prepubescent boys who could be easily dominated physically; (2) the traditional libertine who was "interested in both women and boys, who were prepared to have sex with boys who were prepubescent or pubertal, provided that either their bodies (in the very young) or their effeminacy (in those who were older) made it possible to categorize them as feminine"; (3) men "attracted to early or late adolescent boys (and mainly the latter) whose desire . . . branded them (despite their sometimes being married) as sodomites"; (4) men "who were not conscious of desiring boys of any age or behavior, and who were profoundly upset by men who did, even one suspects, if such men were traditional libertines."[25] This last category, men who could not imagine same-sex contact as masculine contact, is the direct ideological ancestor of modern heterosexuality because for its members, as for many today, "To be masculine was to experience sexual desire only for women."[26] For the post-Restoration subject, masculinity, far from being a social or contextual practice, began to inhere in the subject as his sexuality, regardless of his social circumstance. The same culture that earlier could "imagine" Sedley's lustful and sodomitical posturing as sexual had increasingly little consciousness of same-sex desire as an authentically male practice. In effect, the eighteenth century's collective sexual imagination, so much more constitutive of gendered identity than the "natural" or "essential," suffers a profoundly limiting decline in regard to the male body.

Such transformations in the meaning of male sexuality register literarily as a polemical discourse on the exclusive naturalness of certain sexual practices and identities. By the time we reach Cleland's novels, *Memoirs of a Woman of Pleasure* (1749) and *Memoirs of a Coxcomb* (1751), we find Cleland clearly employing the two principal fictions of natural heterosexuality: the fiction of spontaneity, and the fiction of complementarity. Briefly, the fiction of spontaneity localizes heterosexual desire in the body as an involuntary response to the proper stimulus. Sir William Delamore, the hero of *Memoirs of a Coxcomb*, for example, first experiences his sexuality as an expression of imminent masculinity that manifests itself spontaneously once Delamore reaches the age when desire for women naturally replaces more immature desires. The spontaneity of Delamore's response insures that, first, he never has to search actively for an appropriate sexual object, since that object automatically invokes a proper response in his body, and second, that whatever sexual impulse he feels will qualify as a natural one, since Delamore has no way to intervene consciously in his own sexual desires. Delamore only has to wait until the time is right to act on his mature desire, but desire as such always occurs immediately and involuntarily to signify Delamore's true (and contradictory) individuality as a man. Replacing the Restoration libertine's ambient sexual interest, which is context-dependent and volitional in object choice, Delamore's sexuality becomes an interior quality of personality that only emerges under the proper conditions.

It is true that Delamore's attraction to his female partners might seem as context-dependent as the libertine's, but, in the terms the novel spells out, this is only because one "essence" evokes another in an endless cycle of unmediated interior urges. Neither Delamore nor his love of the moment intend to desire each other. Such "interiority," because it is spontaneous and unmotivated, comes to signify what is most natural about Delamore's masculinity. Delamore's childhood is thus sexualized, but only as an intimation of his mature and unavoidable heterosexuality. Delamore as child is thus radically different from the youthful sodomite whose passivity or effeminacy renders him sexual only in relation to the desire acted out upon his body. In the years between the Restoration and the mid-century, in other words, representations of masculinity and male sexuality concern themselves less and less with subjective volition or activity, and more with an essentially male state of being, so that contextual male sexuality, *precisely because it cannot be made interior to the subject and thus "natural,"* can no longer represent an appropriately masculine subjectivity.

The fiction of complementarity, in its turn, links this newly innate masculine sexuality to its only appropriate object, the female body. By way of complementarity, "male" and "female" become unquestioned mutual referents in a signifying system structured simultaneously by the logic of heterosexual difference and by what we may call the logic of heterosexual synergism. If we examine the logic of difference as Laqueur formulates it, we see that man and woman in the first half of the eighteenth century become distinct physical and sexual entities, and as a result, the terms "male" and "female" come to reflect a profound epistemological divide where gender separates the sphere of eighteenth-century society into categories of the public and private, the domestic and the political, even the passionate and the frigid. Laqueur writes that in the eighteenth century,

> Organs that had shared a name—ovaries and testicles—were now linguistically distinguished. Organs that had not been distinguished by a name of their own—the vagina, for example, were given one. Structures that had been thought common to man and woman—the skeleton and the nervous

system—were differentiated so as to correspond to the cultural male and female. . . .

Woman's purported passionlessness was one of the many possible manifestations of this newly created sex. Female orgasm, which had been the body's signal of successful generation, was banished to the borderlands of physiology, a signifier without a signified.[27]

By reorchestrating "male" and "female," difference signals a fundamental incommensurability between the two sexes that, among its other functions, acts as a limiting influence on spontaneous sexuality by circumscribing the semiotic field in which nature may irrupt. "Women" and "men" may be many things, but in the epistemological model Laqueur describes, they are always something *other* than each other.

This reliable principle of difference is in its turn indispensable to insuring that men and women will invoke each other as sexual and social partners. In the antimasturbatory tract, *Onania; or the Heinous Sin of Self-Pollution* (c. 1708), for example, one of the anonymous narrator's greatest anxieties has to do with masturbatory degradations of male/female difference.[28] *Onania* rests on the fulcrum of the change Laqueur describes: women are ontologically inferior to men, but since they share in the same overarching Galenic system of sexuality that defines male sexuality, their sexual differences are a matter of degree rather than of sexual singularity. At the same time, though, women embody their degree of inferiority to men as a difference that symbolically estranges them from men. Men and women can, in other words, correspond to each other in *Onania*'s sexual economy only as long as their natural variation from each other allows us to construe "similarity" as "inferiority." There must be a significant categorical gap between "similarity" and "identity" to insure the proper sexual hierarchy of English society, and it is this gap that defines sexual difference in *Onania*'s world and that governs any stable interrelation of the two sexes. The danger of female sexuality for *Onania* is that when women masturbate, their masturbatorily enlarged clitorises erode this symbolic difference so that they begin to approximate the male penis. Sexual difference, consequently, ceases to enforce any secure boundary between men and women, with the result that (for the narrator) England's entire social fabric unravels. But the emerging logic of heterosexual difference works so strongly in *Onania*'s sexual hermeneutic that even as women approximate men through masturbation, the tract's narrator can recuperate heterosexual difference by recategorizing masturbating women as hermaphrodites, thus preserving discrete male and female zones on even the perverse body. We find this same conservative logic at work nearly half a century later in the scene of homosexual intercourse Cleland exploits in *Memoirs of a Woman of Pleasure*, where the homosexual male body is made to bear "male" and "female" sites even as Cleland denigrates it for taking part in "same"-sex contact.

Necessarily coupled with this logic of difference, though, is a logic of synergism that reunites female and male as complementary parts of a larger system of sexual and social production. As the rhetoric of heterosexuality becomes more an institution of the early eighteenth century, the difference that defines men and women as separate must be subordinated to an ideology of purpose that aligns male and female teleologically and, most importantly, elicits heterosexual difference as the sign of a greater biological and social communion between the sexes. Sexual difference is requisite to instating true heterosexual economies. *Onania* heralds this shift even as it preserves an older one-sex model expressed as degrees of sexual difference. But whether the heterosexual economy is reproductive, as in *Onania*, or productive of pleasure, as in *Memoirs*, it only becomes possible once the significative play between male and female has been, at least ideally, suspended, and the notion of sexual

difference has been reincorporated as part of a harmonious heterosexual partnership. Difference per se implies no necessary relation
between discrete bodies, but difference as a category with sexual
significance for the eighteenth century mandates that "male" and
"female" refer to each other without pause. Such difference is, in
other words, intelligible only to the extent that it always refers to
some heterosexual imperative beyond difference itself.

I have already discussed *Onania* and *Memoirs of a Coxcomb*
in relation to the historical and literary emergence of a dominant
heterosexual ideology. I want now to give a brief overview of each
chapter and to suggest the theoretical and thematic interrelations
linking these chapters together as a critique of sexual identity in
eighteenth-century English literature. Each of the chapters examines
competing theories of sexual difference and sexual identity in regard to the autonomy and social position of the sexualized subject,
and while the methodological particulars of reading vary from chapter to chapter, I have tried to preserve a consistently critical attitude
toward the truth claims each text makes while at the same time
remaining faithful to the rhetorical structures underlying each work.
    Chapter 1 in many ways lays the groundwork for this project
by introducing sexual difference as a natural correspondence between
men and women that disallows other kinds of sexual and social
interaction. By reading *Onania* for its encrypted anxiety about homosexuality and the potential of homosexual community effected through
a shared discourse of masturbation, this chapter shows how an apparently "natural" heterosexual difference based on nonvolitional sexual
desire must be shored up by *Onania*'s own antimasturbatory discourse.
Onania represents masturbation as an essentially parodic and secondary practice that simultaneously imitates and undercuts the primacy

of heterosexual intercourse, thus appropriating to the individual those pleasures that "naturally" attend only the communal activities of male/female intercourse. And because sexual difference degrades as the subject masturbates, the monstrously homosexual male who progressively replaces "normal" men and women during each masturbatory event in *Onania*'s repertoire typifies all of the anti-Onanist's anxieties about sexual identity and the heterosexual politics of community powering *Onania*'s political economy of desire and reproduction.

In chapter 2, I extend this critique of exclusive communal associations by examining the hermeneutic power that sodomy as an interpretive category exercises in Jonathan Swift's political satires on William Wood, John, Lord Hervey, and Richard Tighe. Each of these men in turn poses a threat to the orderliness of Irish society as Swift conceives it, whether in the guise of Wood's debased copper halfpence, Hervey's Whig ties to Walpole's government, or Tighe's interference in the preferment of Swift's friend, Thomas Sheridan. Significantly, Swift meets that threat by poetically refiguring his rivals as participants in sodomitical dramas that emasculate the enemy and push him beyond the pale of normal society, but what is most telling in Swift's treatment of images of sodomy is that the sexuality of male bodies in Swift's poetry itself serves as a site where personal and private identity enters explicitly into the political order of parliamentary acts and ecclesiastical preferments via the perverse articulation of male sexuality. Male sexuality for Swift, in other words, absorbs political identity and makes the work of good government hinge upon a well-regulated masculine subjectivity. Uncontrolled political associations between men translate directly into the disintegration of Irish and English society unless sodomites like Wood, Hervey, and Tighe are contained satirically. The specifying function that sexual difference performs for other works in this study is thus for Swift internalized by male sexuality, and its differentiating power is transferred to the task of policing normal and perverse masculinities. As a consequence, Swift's satires may employ this internalized sexual difference between true men and sodomites to neutralize their sodomitical targets. Sodomy is always a proscriptive category in the English jurisprudential tradition, and its constitution as a meaningful category of gender, or worse and more specifically of personal identity, always does violence to the subjectivity thus constituted. Swift uses this violence to exclude his political enemies from Irish politics and from the corporate identity of Irish society.

Chapter 3 takes anxieties about the categorical instability of sexual difference one step further by transposing those fears to the level of moral accountability in Alexander Pope's epistles, *To Cobham* (1734) and *To a Lady* (1735). There, the markers of sexual difference become less a matter of physicality and more one of personal character or its lack, but the concept of sexual differentiation still leaves men and women separate and unequal. As I argue, though, Pope exploits the Theophrastan genre of the literary character to effect this differentiation, and in doing so, he opens his studies of male character and female characterlessness to a structural countercritique that continually effaces the difference he attempts to install. In drawing the male characters of *To Cobham*, Pope strategically employs a principle of observation like but not extensive with empirical skepticism to lend authority to his own pronouncements on the nature of masculinity and its accessibility to our understanding. This quasi-empirical principle allows Pope to read male character as consistently inconsistent and thus reliable. Pope also uses this principle of observability to isolate instances of female characterlessness in *To a Lady* as if those instances existed independently in the poet's field of vision instead of as synecdochic and ideologically motivated reductions of feminine experience. If we examine this synecdochic compression, which is central to generic expressions of character and moral identity in both epistles, we find that both male and female subjects depend on the same rhetorical structure and cannot be kept as separate as Pope proposes. Sexual difference thus becomes something Pope's epistles accomplish at the expense of a blindness to the truth of the poems' own figurative constructions.

Chapter 4 considers Eliza Haywood's 1727 novel, *Philidore and Placentia*, as an instance of the changing genre of early-eighteenth-century English romance fiction. Traditionally, Haywood's novel has been interpreted as an unproblematic example of the *chronique scandaleuse*. My reading exposes the heterosexist bias that underlies this tradition and shows how Haywood exploits a character known as the Christian Eunuch to disturb the heterosexual context of the romance genre. Besides reinforcing the orientalist and homoerotic exoticism of Haywood's plot, the Christian Eunuch puts into question the heterosexual ideology underpinning Haywood's main narrative—a love story between Philidore, the handsome young scion of a noble but degenerate line, and his almost impossibly pure and beautiful mistress, Placentia—in two ways. First, the Eunuch presents Philidore with an alternative object of desire to which Philidore will react unpredictably. Philidore is, for example, drawn to the Eunuch with an affection that the novel represents as simultaneously inexplicable and fraternal. Second, the Eunuch's beautiful but damaged body makes him much more like the novel's female characters, whose sexual nature emerges only in opposition to the novel's apparently stable standard of masculinity. The Eunuch's castration reveals the contingent nature of gender identifications normally hidden by the seamless character of Haywood's scandal fiction. These identifications suddenly become visible, put at risk by Haywood's failure to recuperate the Eunuch as a gendered individual. Finally, Haywood employs the Eunuch's castration as a way to contain and to discipline the disruptive presence of the male body in a genre historically associated with a female readership.

Chapter 5, on Cleland's *Memoirs of a Woman of Pleasure* and *Memoirs of a Coxcomb*, explores the naturalization of heterosexual difference and desire. By exploiting the dual fictions of spontaneity and complementarity, Cleland's novels establish a sexuality apparently grounded in corresponding physical differences. "Female" and "male" thus become the privileged interpretive categories for any socially significant relation between individuals, since heterosexuality is a given by which both the naturalness of male/female relations can be calculated and by which the perverseness of nonheterosexual encounters is judged. As I show, though, a series of subordinate oppositions structuring Fanny's relationship with Charles and with Mr. Crofts, such as that between age and youth or between organic and mechanical, comprise Cleland's ideology of the natural, so that what at first appears to the most unmediated expression of spontaneous heterosexuality in reality draws upon these internal oppositions for a rhetorical coherence it cannot by itself claim. Fanny's passion for her beautiful young lover, Charles, allies her sexually with a body much more like her own female form than Cleland's theory of sexual difference alone can support, and Cleland must shore up the priority of heterosexuality by contrasting appropriate heterosexual practices with a scene of homosexual intercourse so similar to the novel's examples of normative heterosexual exchange that sexual difference as an interpretive strategy may be applied meaningfully to what should be the novel's least assimilable episode. Seen in this light, the exclusions Cleland's notions of heterosexuality make possible are less a result of their putative naturalness and more a political manipulation of possible communities. That is, instead of being a benign alternative to heterosexuality, homosexuality becomes heterosexuality's demonic antithesis as the novel endeavors to transform cultural bias into the inevitability of nature.

ONE

Onania: Self-Pollution and the Danger of Female Sexuality

In 1723, the bookseller Thomas Crouch issued the eighth edition of what, if its own testimonials are to be believed, had become one of the most influential pamphlets on the theory and practice of human sexuality to appear in England during the first half of the eighteenth century.[1] This pamphlet, *Onania; or the Heinous Sin of Self-Pollution*, claimed to provide

> Spiritual and Physical Advice to those who have already injured themselves by this abominable Practice. And seasonable Admonition to the *Youth* of this Nation, (of both SEXES) and those whose Tuition they are under, whether *Parents, Guardians, Masters, or Mistresses.*[2]

That *Onania* did indeed have a significant impact on its English, and then on a larger European, audience is apparent from the place it has won in social histories on the period. Lawrence Stone writes:

> The first popular pamphlet which spoke frankly about the terrible moral and physical dangers of masturbation was published in London in about 1710 by an anonymous clergyman.[3]

31

It was entitled *Onania or the Heinous Sin of Self-Pollution, and all its frightful Consequences in both Sexes considered.* Despite its vapid moralizing and implausible stories of resulting disease, the book was a great success. By 1760, thirty-eight thousand copies had been sold in nineteen English editions. It had also been translated into French and German, so that it clearly struck some hidden area of anxiety in early eighteenth-century Europe.[4]

Sander Gilman has observed, "The hypothesis that masturbation was a cause, if not the prime cause, of insanity was first promulgated in the anonymous English moral tractate *Onania; or the Heinous Sin of Self-Pollution,*"[5] and Gilman cites the work of René A. Spitz, who sees *Onania* as instituting a telling change in European attitudes toward masturbation and its social significance:

> In secular literature the subject [of masturbation] is mentioned for the first time after the Romans by Rousseau. In the interval, a momentous change in the attitude toward masturbation had taken place. The change was initiated by the first moralistic publication devoted exclusively to the subject, a pamphlet published in England, *Onania*, attributed to one Dekker, probably of Dutch origin.[6]

The change Spitz has in mind is one affecting masturbation's possible construction as, variously, a moral, pathological, or legal entity. According to Spitz, masturbation moves from being either an emission "to be cleansed like any excretion" or a transgression that "entails the least severe penance of any sexual misdemeanor"[7] to being a practice that

> In Women . . . if frequently practis'd, relaxes and spoils the retentive Faculty, occasions the *Fluor albus*, an obnoxious

as well as perplexing Illness attending that Sex, which upon
account of the Womb, may draw on a whole Legion of Dis-
orders, it makes 'em look pale, and those who are not of a
good Complexion, swarthy and haggard. (19–20)

Female masturbation also causes

Hysteric Fits, and sometimes, by draining away all the radical
Moistures, *Consumption*. But what it more often produces
than either is *Barrenness*, and at length a total ineptitude to
the Act of Generation it self; Misfortunes very afflicting to
them, because seldom to be redress'd. (20)

Not only does the masturbating woman despoil herself with hysteria,
tuberculosis, and infertility—the hallmark diseases of eighteenth-
century antimasturbatory discourse—she also loses the pleasures and
social position associated with English motherhood. Her "unredress-
able" barrenness prevents her, for example, from experiencing the
social satisfaction that attaches to

a Man at the Age of Fourscore, with a Wife of the like An-
tiquity, both bless'd with healthy hail Constitutions, and
fresh wholesome Countenances, with sound Minds, and per-
fect Senses, with active Limbs, and of chearful Tempers,
[who preside] *over a healthful Progeny, perhaps to the third*
or fourth Generation. (19)

Rather than taking her place in a community defined by "natural"
heterosexual intercourse, the masturbating woman instead becomes
an alienated object under the scrutiny of this community:

[I]f we turn our Eyes upon licentious Masturbaters, we shall
find them with meagre Jaws, and pale Looks, with feeble

Hams, and Legs without Calves, their Generative Faculties weaken'd, if not destroy'd in the Prime of their Years. A Jest to others, and a Torment to themselves. (19)

Man and woman serve as physical and moral counterparts in a system that must be able to identify and utilize the difference between male and female. Paradoxically, men and women who respect the proper sexual difference grow more and more alike: sexual difference here expresses itself as a set of mutual similarities in constitution, countenance, mind, and temper that unite the two sexes in a synergistic whole, whereas the anti-Onanist's negative symptomatology reduces both male and female masturbators to the same debased reproductive state. This elision of sexual difference even in healthy heterosexual couples would seem to implicate the anti-Onanist's ideal as thoroughly in gender ambiguity as masturbation does, but since true sexual difference for the anti-Onanist inheres in the oppositional relation of "Man" to "Wife," no "licentious Masturbater" can meet the criteria of difference *Onania* demands. Consequently, as the terms "Man" and "Wife" drop away, men and women alike become the same pale, slack-jawed, knock-kneed "Jest" characteristic of masturbation. Masturbation thus endangers sexual difference; it draws an ominous equation between male and female that homogenizes the sexual body and, as we will see, transforms heterosexual difference into homosexual proximity.

The female body is, I will contend, the principal episteme of heterosexual anxiety in *Onania*. When *Onania*'s presumptive male author describes the effect masturbation has on the early-eighteenth-century female body, he installs a difference between normal and perverse female sexuality that is, in its turn, a displacement of the "natural" difference between male and female sexualities. The anti-Onanist thus produces a text that makes us question the sex of the voice we hear once we begin to read his words and to piece together a complicated gender puzzle equating the masturbating eighteenth-century woman with the emerging category of the monstrous homosexual man. The anti-Onanist's anxiety about stable sexual difference centers, I argue, on the figure of the masturbating woman for two reasons. First, masturbation as a parody of community-building heterosexual intercourse produces its own subject as an indecorous approximation of the heterosexual ideal. Second, the masturbating woman who thus isolates herself from heterosexual society so successfully parodies the masculine subject that she both violates that subject and renders "his" difference from "her" meaningless. I will use this chapter to examine briefly the parodic relation through which masturbation as an antisocial practice conserves, and through that conservation subverts, the communal dimension of heterosexual intercourse, and I will show how masturbatory female sexuality undermines any stable notion of sexual difference by eroding the binary referents of *Onania*'s heterosexual system.

To define masturbation as a "heinous sin," the anti-Onanist must first invoke a correspondence between male and female bodies marked by communal purpose. The closest we ever come to an explicit definition of masturbation is the following:

> SELF-POLLUTION is that unnatural Practice, by which Persons of either Sex, may defile their own Bodies, without the Assistance of others, whilst yielding to filthy Imaginations, they endeavour to imitate and procure to themselves that Sensation, which God has order'd to attend the carnal Commerce of the two Sexes, for the Continuance of our Species. (1)

This passage provides little real information either about actual masturbatory practices or about heterosexual intercourse. It cannot, for instance, tell us which "Sensation" attends "the carnal Commerce of the two sexes" or which sensations make masturbation a poor copy of another kind of activity. Masturbation *imitates* heterosexual intercourse through its association with the "filthy" but otherwise unspecified "imaginations" by which masturbators try to copy a more natural form of intercourse, but masturbation itself can only be considered *parodic* if heterosexual intercourse already exists as a normative category controlling any instance of unclean "imaginations." According to the anti-Onanist, people masturbate to imitate an action that, in many of the cases cited in *Onania*, they have never known and cannot know because of their masturbatorily induced disabilities. But the entire category of parodic masturbation must incorporate an already existing notion of heterosexual coitus if masturbation is to be made reliably inferior to, and so parodic of, the "carnal Commerce" that defines the public sphere of reproductive intercourse. "Male" and "female" consequently function as corresponding semiotic limits for each other while simultaneously recuperating masturbatory sexuality as an individual attempt to copy a communal activity distinguished by its ontological priority. Identifying heterosexual "Commerce" as the origin for imitative masturbatory sensations thus makes defining masturbation doubly difficult: actual masturbation may or may not refer to heterosexual practices, but no understanding of masturbatory pleasure is possible without this preexisting notion of heterosexual intercourse to undergird the parodic hierarchy of sexual practices. We cannot, in other words, know what sensations parodic masturbation produces, only what it imitates. Masturbation by this logic is never an original practice itself, but rather a parodic derivation that conserves the very heterosexual system it appears to threaten.

In effect, the masturbator substitutes herself for the more appropriate object of desire. In *Onania*'s sexual hierarchy, both the desire that motivates masturbation and the masturbatory activity itself literally displace the appropriate subject of sexual attention onto the masturbator's own body: the subject, that is, never really masturbates for pleasure. Instead, one substitutively takes on the character of another's body, which in its role as sexual object already occurs in the domain of public sexuality and which is the proper recipient of the masturbator's misplaced attentions. So women who masturbate, especially virgins, find that they may, according to the anti-Onanist,

> by being heedless, or perhaps more fill'd with impure de-sires than ordinary, actually deflower themselves, and fool-ishly part with that valuable Badge of their Chastity and Innocence, which when once lost, is never to be retriev'd. This may be the fatal Cause whenever they Marry, of end-less Jealousies and Family Quarrels, and make their Hus-bands suspect more than they have deserv'd, wrongfully imagining, that there is but one Way by which Maids may forfeit their Virginity. (20)

The masturbating woman places herself in a male position in relation to her own body, thus giving herself an effectively doubled sexual identity. By assuming her husband's position, she "deflowers" herself and usurps the husband's prerogative, but since her body remains the identifiably "female" site where this masculine usurpa-tion occurs, the masturbating woman effectively homosexualizes her contact with herself and consequently indulges in a masturbatory form of tribadism. Her husband, on the other hand, slights mastur-bation's deconstructive power by suspecting his wife of infidelity with another man when he should rightly suspect her of infidelity with her own masculinized self. The woman's actions cannot be pleasurable because for *Onania*, pleasure (or at least the divinely ordained "Sensation" of carnal commerce) by definition belongs only to monogamous heterosexual intercourse. To approximate pleasure, therefore, is to approximate heterosexuality masturbatorily and poorly. In the anti-Onanist's epistemology of masturbatory sexuality, the masturbator objectifies her own body by using it to procure an inappropriate knowledge of another's position, not pleasure.

This anxiety over female sexuality motivates much of the anti-Onanist's diatribe against "self-pollution." The relationship between masturbation and female identity that unfolds in the *Supplement* makes this anxiety especially clear and prompts the anti-Onanist to an important extended meditation on the social effects of masturbatory female sexuality. The particular occasion for this meditation is a remarkable letter from a young woman who has learned about masturbation from a female servant and who, at the time of writing, has developed a terrifying problem:

> I began, Sir, the folly at 11 Years of Age, was taught it by my Mother's Chamber Maid, who lay with me from that Time all along till now, which is full seven Years, and so intimate were we in the Sin, that we took all Opportunities of committing it, and invented all the ways we were capable of to highten the Titillation, and gratifie our sinful Lusts the more. We, in short, pleasured one another, as well as each our selves, but whether by the hard usage of my Parts by her, or my self, or both, or whether from any thing in Nature more in my make, than is customary to the Sex, I don't know, but for above half a Year past I have had a Swelling that thrusts out from my body, as big, and almost as hard, and as long or longer than my Thumb, which inclines me to excessive lustful Desires, and from it their [*sic*] issues a moisture or slipp'riness to that degree that I am almost continually wet, and sometimes have such a forcing, as if something of a large Substance was coming from me, which greatly frightens both me and my Maid. (*Supplement*, 152)

The anti-Onanist's answer to this woman taps into an ancient epistemology of human sexuality that proves decisive in articulating the interrelation between masturbation and homosexuality:

This young Lady's Case, through the height of her Lust, and force and frequency of abusing herself, and probably the unnatural propendance of the Part, is no more, according to the Account she gives, than a relaxation of the *Clitoris*, a thing common to many of the Sex, both in the single and married, who are Vigorous and Lustful, and have given up themselves to the Practice of *Self-Pollution* for any time. In some Women it extends it self, and is enlarged when inflated to the exact likeness and size of a human *Penis* erect, except that it has no perforation, (though it really looks, by the natural Impression at the end, as if there was a Passage) nor is altogether so long, but yet it erects and falls as that does, in proportion to the venereal Desire or Inclination of the Woman. (*Supplement*, 154)

To support his diagnosis, the anti-Onanist then quotes verbatim a letter from *Dr. Carr's Medicinal Epistles* about two nuns in Rome who were reputed to have changed sex.[8] Dr. Carr opines:

WHOSOEVER thinks that those two *Nuns* have changed their Sex, is under a Mistake; all that gives any Ground for such an Opinion, is, the uncommon Encrease of the *Clitoris*, which as it is used to frequent Irritations, thrusts out and enlarges its Dimensions, not unlike to a human *Penis*. (*Supplement*, 157–58)

Dr. Carr also informs us that

THIS uncommon Growth of the *Clitoris,* is so frequent in some Eastern Countries, that the most skilful Chirurgeons, have found out a Method of amputating it; and to take it away from Persons about to marry, lest it should be a hinderance in *Coition*. (*Supplement*, 159)

The "uncommon Growth" of the supposedly female clitoris, an increase so common as to have deserved its own medical literature and castrating surgical procedures, is in fact one realization of female sexual potential inherent in the Galenic model of sexuality at work here. Thomas Laqueur, in his "Orgasm, Generation, and the Politics of Reproductive Biology," writes:

> For several thousand years it had been a commonplace that women have the same genitals as men, except that, as Nemesius, bishop of Emesa in the sixth century, put it: 'Theirs are inside the body and not outside it.' Galen, who in the second century A.D. developed the most powerful and resilient model of the homologous nature of male and female reproductive organs, could already cite the anatomist Herophilus (third century B.C.) in support of his claim that a woman has testes with accompanying seminal ducts very much like the male's, one on each side of the uterus, the only difference being that the male's are contained in the scrotum and the female's are not.[9]

Compare this passage to Dr. Carr's comments:

> Further, Sir, upon a Comparison of the Male and Female Organs, you will not find them to differ so much as you imagine at first Appearance, excepting, that those of a Man are thrust out with a more vigorous Heat; whereas those of a Woman by a defect in that Respect, are only to be perceived inwardly.
>
> The *Uterus* of a Woman, upon turning out, would resemble a *Scrotum*, and the two Ovaries annex'd to the sides of its Bottom, with what they include, would make up the Number of the *Testicles*.
>
> The *Clitoris* is shaped like a *Penis*; it has the same Sense

of Pleasure, and stretches out, and relaxes in the same manner again; it also ends in a Gland, but wants a Cavity; which is no wonder, because it does not serve for the discharge of any thing, as it ouzes out its Contents more conveniently into the Apperture of the Neck of the Bladder; but was that Apperture to be closed, as it is in Men, then, in an Erection, it would necessarily find some other outlet towards the end of its Gland. (*Supplement*, 160)

Carr also notes that the irritated clitoris grows "BECAUSE the fury of Lust, wonderfully distends the Nerves and Arteries, and particularly, above any other Parts, blows up those Organs with Spirits and Heat" (*Supplement*, 159). For his part, Laqueur writes that

Heat is of critical importance in the Galenic account. It is, to begin with, the sign of perfection, of one's place in the hierarchical great chain of being. Humans are the most perfect of animals, and men are more perfect than women by reason of their "excess of heat." Men and women are, in this model, not different in kind but in the configuration of their organs; the male is a hotter version of the female, or to use the teleologically more appropriate order, the female is the cooler, less perfect version of the male. (4)

Inasmuch as a variation in "heat" marks off male from female bodies, this difference in degree should function effectively to preserve the biological boundary between male and female that in its turn reassures us of the difference between socially "masculine" and "feminine" practices. *Onania* rests on the fulcrum of the relation Laqueur describes: women are ontologically inferior to men, but since they share in the same overarching Galenic system of sexuality that defines male sexuality, female sexual differences are a matter of degree rather than of sexual singularity or absolute difference.

At the same time, though, women embody their degree of differ-ence as a difference that must symbolically estrange them from men. Men and women correspond to each other in *Onania*'s sexual economy only as long as their natural variation from each other allows us to construe "similarity" as "inferiority." But to admit the strangeness or pervasive difference of the clitorally enlarged woman from her clitorally "normal" counterpart, as the anti-Onanist and his medical authorities do, is to allow masturbation an important homosexualizing tendency and to admit the fear of homosexuality and of the fall of reliable biological boundaries that mobilize that masturbatory anxiety in the first place.[10] After all, to call a clitorally enlarged woman "different," or to admit that her organ has "the exact likeness and size of a human *Penis* erect," is to marginalize her sexuality in the same way that masturbatory sexuality in *Onania* is marginalized, but it is also to admit the way in which the clitorally enlarged woman's organ mimics the "male" penis and positions her and her possible desires as homosexual. Conversely, to identify this woman's enlarged organ as still a clitoris is to reassure, but it is also to install the potentially homosexualizing difference of this organ as part of her normative female sexuality. In other words, we have to be told repeatedly that the penislike clitoris is just that, a clitoris, and no matter how often we run across this sort of organ (or what the organ is doing when we encounter it), its incidence is always reassuringly "unusual."[11]

To understand exactly how *Onania*'s masturbating women re-late to the question of homosexuality, we must first understand how female masturbation opens the female body to a number of destabilizing reclassifications. We should, for instance, ask how it is that women who possess a natural female organ like the clitoris, which exists in an enlarged but still identifiably female state and is subject to the heat of salacious but unspecified[12] desires, end up being classified as hermaphroditic.[13] The woman whose clitoris has been enlarged masturbatorily is, we find, "able to perform the

Actions of Men with other Women" (*Supplement*, 163), and this discussion of abnormal *female* sexuality segues immediately to one of hermaphroditism in an apparently causal fashion. The narrator reports:

> I have read, that in *France*, there are a People, who have a great propension of the *Clitoris*, naturally, and are equally able to make use of those of both Sexes, and that the Laws there, leave to their Choice, which Sex to make use of, after which, the use of the other are absolutely forbidden them. (*Supplement*, 163)

Heterosexuality seems for *les Français(es)* to be less a naturally instated phenomenon than a statutorily enforced regulation. French hermaphroditism in *Onania*'s account displaces our modern notion of the hermaphrodite as an individual with reliably distinct male and female sexual organs with a more difficult categorical asymmetry. This passage suggests that an entire people's sexual identity is at some fundamental level determined by an unproblematically female clitoris, the identity of which somehow conditions the organs of both sexes without obliterating sexual difference. But the point is that this sexual difference only functions as such after a legally motivated decision. For at least part of a subject's life, the clitoris thus permeates both male and female sexuality, producing a sexuality that is equally indeterminate and female at the same time. There is no hetero- or homosexuality before choice and the law intervene; the moment of intervention, though, is significantly a prohibition of any homosexuality, so that law and homosexuality bring each other into existence when the possible resolutions of an individual's gender identity become most imminent. French law thus rules homosexuality out of existence as the only possible example of gender indeterminacy.[14] It is no accident that these passages, which essentially interpret the clitoris as the female penis, lead easily into stories of truly monstrous hermaphroditic sexuality.[15] If an enlarged clitoris (but enlarged in relation to what standard?) is indeed a feminine phenomenon as well as a monstrous phenomenon, then it makes sense that discussions of clitoral sexuality can fit interchangeably into discussion of monstrous hermaphroditism:

> And we read that in *Florida*, there is a Nation, which have the Generative Parts of both Sexes; To confirm the same, those that will take the pains to consult the Works of *Jacobus de Moyne*, may see a Description of them, in certain Figures; but it seems they are a People that are hated by the very *Indians*, and by them made servile, to carry Burdens, and do Offices instead of Beasts, they being very strong and able Bodied. *Plauterus* says, he saw a *Clitoris* in a Woman, as big and as long as the Neck of a Goose. *Riolanus* and *Schenkius*, two noted Physicians, both say, they have observed it as long in a Woman as a Man's Finger. *Plempius* writes of one *Helena*, a Woman, that lay with several Women, and vitiated several Virgins with that Part. *Diemerbroek* says, he himself saw, in a certain Woman at *Montfort*, a *Clitoris*, as long and thick as the ordinary *Penis* of a Man, which came to be of that magnitude, after she had lain-in, three or four times. (*Supplement*, 163–64)

The epistemological oddness of this paragraph comes in part from its own categorical inconsistency. On the one hand, women with enlarged clitorises are still perfectly recognizable as women, different from real men who possess authentic penises. On the other hand, these women slip just as easily into the categorically unstable roles of hermaphrodites, lesbians, foreigners, the colonized, and most dangerously, monstrous homosexual men. Take, for instance, the Venetian Courtesan whose large and bony clitoris "by reason of its extream hardness, did so hurt her Lovers, in *Coition*, that many times, by reason of Inflammations thereby, they were forced to fly to the Surgeons for help" (*Supplement*, 165). Are these "Inflammations" related to heat, that sign of teleologically perfect masculinity in the Galenic system of sexual differentiation? Does the woman's bony clitoris displace the proper male penis during intercourse and thereby damage that penis by inflaming it? Does the woman's clitoris, itself inflamed with venereal desire, become a penis in its own right and thus involve the more naturally proper man and his penis in a scene of homosexual intercourse? Does a woman who approximates a man still remain a woman and thus enter into a homosexual liaison whenever she couples with another woman? If something looks like a penis and acts like a penis, how can one person pretend to possess a superior organ or one that is more authentic than someone else's? In effect, the anti-Onanist argues that the masturbating eighteenth-century woman transforms her own body so as to make it impossible for a "real" man ever to claim either the phallus's symbolic power entirely for himself or even to claim that his own penis is reliably different from those monstrous other penises he may meet with during his sexual peregrinations.[16] The anti-Onanist tells us:

> MONTUUS, *de Med. Thores. Lib. 1. cap.6.* says, that a certain Hermophrodite, who was counted to be a Woman, was married, bore Sons and Daughters, and notwithstanding was wont to lie with her Maids and get them with Child. I have read a remarkable Account of an Hermophrodite, in a certain City in *Scotland*, that went for a Maid, yet got her Master's Daughter, who lay in the same Bed with her, with Child: She was accused of the Fact, in the Year 1461, found capable, as Man as well as Woman, convicted, and condemn'd before the Judges, and suffered Death, by being put into the Ground alive. (*Supplement*, 165–66)

One categorical violation, that of "male" by "female," must be punished by another, that of "life" by "death." This Scottish man/maid's execution restores the epistemological stability of heterosexual society over the destabilizing, potentially homosexualizing activity of the hermaphrodite. After all, this passage considers its subject a woman even as it variously renders that subject's actions as male or female, since "She was . . . found capable, as Man as well as Woman." As far abroad as all of these discussions of perverse, monstrous female, and exotic foreign sexuality wander, they are all part of the anti-Onanist's masturbatory symptomatology. Simply put, masturbation acts as the epistemological link between homosexuality and hermaphroditism: frequent masturbation in the female heats and irritates that body to the point where it approximates the male body. In the Galenic system, this ontological shift is always a one-way move towards a more nearly male (and thus more nearly perfect) state. In *Onania*'s sexual epistemology, the masturbatory transformation of female into male results in a monstrous proximity of male and female that obliterates heterosexual categories and leaves the man open to the "danger" of possible homosexual encounters. The phallic woman constitutes such a source of anxiety because "she" is doubly proximate. She preserves the epistemological characteristics of both masculinity and femininity, and her desire is thus unpredictable and inevitably homosexualizing: every sexual contact she experiences requires her to displace some element of the heterosexual matrix with the all too similar traits of her multiply sexed body. This contact is especially disastrous when it takes place within the supposedly normalizing bonds of a heterosexual relationship (like marriage), or even when contact between individuals begins to look as if it could approach such a normative state. This is why the Scottish man/maid, whose activities could make her look like a husband or lover if we didn't know better, is such a threat to Scottish society. The masturbating woman can be many things, all of them wrong, and most of them particularly dangerous when she can no longer be relied upon to be female. She is truly a categorical nightmare.[17]

The most prominent anxiety about masturbatory sexuality in *Onania* is, as it turns out, part of a larger concern with the interrelation of sexual activity and political community. The fear that masturbatory sexuality (a sexuality that may afflict any subject regardless of race, religion, class, or sex) will put an end to the heterosexual means of social production by perverting existing families and diverting potential family members from their true purpose is itself coupled to, and in an important sense derives from, a concern with masturbation's transformative capacity. Masturbatory sexuality, as we have seen, radically alters the individual body, which "naturally" belongs to the sphere of public, reproductive heterosexuality. Masturbation is thus a parodic and failed form of heterosexual intercourse whereby the subject replaces an appropriately different object with her own body and transforms her body into that of the appropriate sexual partner. This substitution conserves the attributes of an "original" heterosexual complementarity while perversely displacing the communal components of heterosexual intercourse onto the masturbator's own body. "True" heterosexual community as a consequence finds itself replaced by the false community of the masturbator's body, but more importantly, the degree of difference that safeguards separate male and female identities erodes and leaves potential sexual partners uncertain as to their place in what should be both a naturally and divinely ordained, and thus unproblematic, activity. This fear that homosexuality, working through masturbatory mechanisms, will uproot and eradicate the possibility of a publicly condoned heterosexuality culminates in the epistemological terror of the masculinized, homosexual, phallic woman. Precisely because she carries within herself and upon her body the suspended but unnegated social and physical markers of the two sexes, the phallic woman is a perfect vehicle for trapping real men with real penises in radically nonproductive homosexual encounters that both endanger and appropriate the very member that should give real Englishmen their authenticity. *Onania* places this disastrous possibility at the heart of its fascination with masturbatory sexuality, but the real terror of masturbation lies not so much in the transitory acts themselves as in the effect those acts must have. Masturbation is what anyone may do here and now, but its true effect lies somewhere within a range of potential consequences that it inaugurates and that exists just beyond the anti-Onanist's anxious heterosexual horizon, in a world where a proper heterosexuality may not be the inevitable consequence of its own practices.

T W O

Swift and the
Political Anus

In the last chapter, we saw how *Onania*'s version of masturbation encodes the possibility of homosexuality and, consequently, of perverse communal association. Masturbatory associations inevitably disrupt the normative heterosexual organization of early-eighteenth-century British society because neither male nor female identities may be reliably safeguarded from masturbatory reconfiguration. The monstrous homosexual man thus becomes, at least for the anti-Onanist, both the agent and the end point of a process of social disintegration that, if left unchecked, brings about the end of productive English society. The figure of the homosexual man, in other words, acts as a terrifying, chaotic image against which heterosexual practices appear in their full necessity. For Jonathan Swift, the homosexual man also serves as a focal point for political and communal identity, but unlike the anti-Onanist, Swift exploits this figure and the discourse of sodomy that enables it to reintegrate political communities around the abused body of the sodomite.

When Swift first poetically engages his political enemy William

Wood in 1724, the worst thing he does to Wood (besides imagine his death) is to bugger him in verse.[1] Swift likens Wood to a statue of a saint and uses Wood's reaction to the "boring" he receives as a mark of the coiner's authenticity:

> A joiner to fasten a saint in a niche,
> Bored a large auger-hole in the image's breech;
> But finding the statue to make no complaint,
> He would ne'er be convinced it was a true saint:
> When the true Wood arrives, as he soon will no doubt,
> (For that's but a sham Wood they carry about)
> What stuff he is made on you quickly may find,
> If you make the same trial, and bore him behind;
> I'll hold you a groat, when you wimble his bum,
> he'll bellow as loud as a de'il in a drum.
>
> $(71-80)^2$

Swift's engagement with Wood and with Walpole's government, both in his own person and in the person of the Drapier, is usually considered his most potent political victory.[3] While "A Serious Poem Upon William Wood" is not the only verse attack Swift launches against Wood, it is the first, and it satirizes and violates Wood in a manner characteristic of the political poems that I will examine. This passage in particular suggests that sodomitical penetration finds out the "truth" about Swift's devilish political enemy in the same way it shows the truth about a false "saint" who makes no complaint when sodomized. Swift leaves open the question of what we use to "bore" Wood's bum, but, as we will see, the activity itself proves a potent hermeneutics for understanding the man's true relation to the Irish.

Swift's treatment of deviant and marginalized sexualities has for the most part been engulfed by the flood of interest in his scatological poems, especially as those poems apparently recuperate a

natural and harmonious heterosexuality from out of their own perverse subject matter.[4] Anal eroticism in his verse has been read repeatedly and exclusively as a corollary of excretion. Indeed, the
most famous essay on Swift and anality, Norman O. Brown's "The
Excremental Vision," interprets "the anal function" as decisively
excremental. Brown opens his essay by opposing the Rabelaisian
or Aristophanic high cultural equivalent of "love me, love my anus"
to Swift's aggressive anality:

> Any reader of Jonathan Swift knows that in his analysis of
> human nature there is an emphasis on, and attitude toward
> the anal function that is unique in Western literature. In
> mere quantity of scatological imagery he may be equaled
> by Rabelais and Aristophanes; but whereas for Rabelais and
> Aristophanes the anal function is part of the total human
> being which they make us love because it is part of life, for
> Swift it becomes the decisive weapon in his assault on the
> pretensions, the pride, even the self-respect of mankind.[5]

Brown elaborates his thesis by arguing:

> The understanding of Swift therefore begins with the rec-
> ognition that Swift's anatomy of human nature, in its en-
> tirety and at the most profound and profoundly disturbing
> level, can be called "The Excremental Vision." (179)

Brown locates anal eroticism most clearly in Swift's Yahoos and
goes on to argue in Freudian fashion that excremental anality, because
it *is* excremental, assimilates the eroticism of human sexuality:

> But if we measure Swift's correctness not by the conven-
> tional and complacent prejudices in favor of human pride
> . . . but by the ruthless wisdom of psychoanalysis, then it is

quite obvious that the excremental vision of the Yahoo is substantially identical with the psychoanalytical doctrine of the extensive role of anal eroticism in the formation of human culture. (190–91)

Brown's essay, first published in 1959, has largely set the tone for studying what have become known as the "scatological" poems.[6] As a consequence, those poems which deal with excremental anal eroticism now stand, critically, for all expressions of anal eroticism in Swift's works, while the few but suggestive gestures towards an anal eroticism other than the excremental kind have received little critical attention. My project here will be, in contrast, to show how Swift's representations of perverse anal sexuality encode sodomy as a potent and satirical political force capable of encompassing both male and female figures. By imputing sodomitical interest or activity to his political rivals, Swift not only contains those rivals, he also creates a complex poetic network where gender identity, perverse sexuality, and masculine politics so intertwine that male sexual identity in Swift's poetry becomes a dangerously unstable source of political power.

This chapter uses the discourse of sodomy to question the prevalent assumption that the politics of shit is the only politics of the anus available to readers of Swift's work in general, and of his poems in particular. My engagement with Swift therefore depends upon two principal tenets: first, that Swift had access to a discourse of sodomy that was itself a potent form of ideological coercion, enforcing as it did a moral, legal, and religious closure of bodily boundaries, zones, and stimuli, and, second, that reading Swift's poems for the effects of this sodomitical discourse powerfully defamiliarizes the traditional ethics and dynamics of sexual identity at work in his satires. Such defamiliarization provides us not just with a visible continuum of same-sex desires and activities otherwise occluded by more general "scatological" sexuality, but also with a more sensitive model for the acquisition of gendered and sexual status in Swift's satiric politics.[7]

We have seen in the introduction how "sodomy" as a legal term receives its first and fullest definition in the work of the seventeenth-century English jurist, Sir Edward Coke. Coke's *Third Part of the Institutes of the Laws of England*, which was completed in 1628, labels "sodomy" as "buggery" and specifies the following criminal activity:

> So as there must be *penetratio*, that is *res in re*, either with mankind or with beast, but the least penetration maketh it carnall knowledge.[8]

This notoriously ambiguous definition cannot, strictly speaking, be confined to sexual acts. Put another way, no act involving *penetratio res in re* can ever be made reliably nonsexual, so that the number of possible transgressions falling under Henry VIII's felony statue becomes practically infinite. Coke reviews historical opinions of sodomy as a crime and finishes his statement with a particular legal finding:

> Our ancient Authors doe conclude, that it deserveth death, *ultimum supplicium*, though they differ in the manner of the punishment. Britton saith, that Sodomites and Miscreants shall be burnt, and so were the Sodomites by Almighty God. Fleta saith, *Pecorantes & Sodomitiae in terra vivi confodiantur:* and therewith agreeth with the Mirror, *pur le grand abomination*, and in another place he saith, *Sodomie est crime de Majestie, vers le Roy celestre*. But (to say it once for all) the judgment in all cases of felony is that the person attainted be hanged by the neck, until he or she be dead.[9]

In theory, sodomy as a criminal practice may refer to almost any site or activity, but by Swift's time the general understanding was that "sodomy" referred primarily to anal penetration,[10] and that the legal injunction against sodomy proscribed certain bodily sites such as the genitals, and especially the anus, for any contact or stimulation other than that of excretion.[11] The anus thus becomes by Swift's time the definitive zone for natural and unnatural contacts, pleasures, and, for Swift, identities.

This overlap of competing ideologies for the "natural" and "unnatural" is, for example, where we find Swift when, in the fourth book of his *Travels* (1726), Gulliver tries to explain human anatomy and medicine to his Houyhnhnm master:

> For Nature (as the Physicians alledge) having intended the superior anterior Orifice only for the *Intromission* of Solids and Liquids, and the inferior Posterior for Ejection; these Artists ingeniously considering that in all Diseases Nature is forced out of her Seat; therefore to replace her in it, the Body must be treated in a Manner directly contrary, by interchanging the Use of each orifice; forcing Solids and Liquids in at the *Anus*, and making Evacuations at the Mouth.[12]

As with many passages of Swiftian satire, this episode ironically disables its own stable interpretation. If, for example, Gulliver's remarks are intended to satirize English physicians and their medical practices, then Gulliver simultaneously ironizes the heterosexually favorable category of "Nature" as a tendentious construct of the medical profession and calls into question the natural propriety of using our "superior anterior Orifice" solely for the "Intromission of Solids and Liquids" or for using the "inferior Posterior" solely "for Ejection." This model for oral intromission and anal ejection stands as natural only so long as Gulliver's reading of the physicians' allegation can be taken unironically. Gulliver's definition of anal and oral propriety is analogous in its ambiguity to Coke's stricture on sodomy; indeed, Gulliver's reading of natural orality and anality could itself stand in for Coke's proscription, since what Gulliver describes certainly conforms to the required *penetratio res in re*. Worse, if Gulliver does speak ironically of the physicians' allegation that solids go in at the mouth and out at the anus, not the other way around, his irony opens a conceptual space for sodomy in the Nature he is busy fabricating. Moreover, by aligning mouth and anus as bodily "orifices" with theoretically exchangeable uses, Gulliver undermines the hierarchy preserving naturally superior and inferior sites. If, after all, the mouth may be made to eject and the anus to admit unnamed (perhaps unnameable) solids, then neither will function reliably as the other's superior counterpart.

The "unnatural" reversibility of this bodily process also implies that "natural" corporeal hierarchies are in themselves inadequate protection against their own overthrow or intentional subversion and that once a hierarchy like Nature's has been overthrown, sacrosanct bodily openings can intentionally be substituted for each other, regardless of natural law. That the doctors' cultural intervention in bodily functions may facilitate natural physical activities like consumption and excretion has nothing to do with the physical possibility of intervention per se, and if one type of intervention is possible, why not another?

All of this takes place as part of an ostensibly medical, and therefore authorizable, procedure for forcing Nature back into her proper seat, but the capacious indeterminacy informing both Gulliver's narrative and Coke's statute makes it impossible to exclude sexuality, and especially perverse sexuality, from Swift's satiric discourse. It is, for example, possible to categorize Gulliver's natural bodily hierarchy of mouth and anus, whether ironically or unironically intended, as a constituent element of those perverse practices which are so peculiar to Gulliver's cultured world and which outrank even indigenous Yahoo obscenities:

> I expected every Moment, that my Master would ac-
> cuse the *Yahoos* of those unnatural Appetites in both Sexes,
> so common among us. But Nature it seems hath not been
> so expert a School-mistress; and these politer Pleasures are
> entirely the Productions of Art and Reason, on our Side of
> the Globe. (230)

Only a subverted natural hierarchy can allow "those unnatural
Appetites in both Sexes" to emerge in their full contrariety, and
invoking as they do the hierarchically encoded and therefore
sodomizable anal and oral zones of "natural bodies," such "appetites" cannot help but signify as part of a Swiftian discourse of
sodomy. Swift may not intend these appetites as sodomitical, but
the genius of the term is its rapacious inclusiveness. The sodomitical context in which Swift's satire takes place would thus be one
where both men and women were capable of sodomizing and being sodomized in a variety of ways. As a consequence, sodomy has
a significant impact on the kind of meaning we may assign to the
deviant characters we find in Swift's work, since in the light of the
history of sodomy, historical characters like William Wood cease
simply to be the humorous butts of Swift's political satires. Instead,
as we will see, these characters become the medium through which
sexuality enters into and structures the political environment.

Consequently, when Swift exploits an image of anal penetration to sharpen his 1724 attack on Wood, he is making use of a
long-standing moral and legal tradition that anathematizes the anus
and makes its stimulation by any means a highly ideologically
charged maneuver. This ideological charge does not reduce to the
language of scatology even when Swift allies sodomitical and excremental images in the same satire; Swiftian sodomy thus requires
attention to its own literary and historical specificity. Swift's scenes
of anal stimulation that feature the penis, the mouth and tongue,
or even the nose, and phallic substitutes like the Irish joiner's auger,

incorporate his writings as part of the sodomitical discourse of prohibited and indeterminate sexual activities that had been statutorily invoked as perverse since Henry VIII. Sodomy as a discourse fundamentally generative of sexual acts that themselves become political identities thus helps to place Swift's political satires in the larger historical context of homosocial male homophobia.

Wood's status as male in "A Serious Poem" is, for example, both an assumption necessary to the poem's sodomitical violence and an assumption that this same violence necessarily rewrites. "A Serious Poem" has usually been read as a virtuoso exercise in Swiftian word games, where Swift organizes a galaxy of disparate but unflattering images simply by punning on Wood's last name.[13] A. B. England articulates this line of reasoning when he argues in his reading of "A Serious Poem" that

> In the poem as a whole, the sequences of images is wildly, exuberantly miscellaneous, lacking any coordinating factors other than the word "wood" and an adaptability to the expression of Swift's anger; the first of these factors provides only a fortuitous verbal connection rather than any thematic relationship, and the second is not a cohesive force because the poem is in large part a demonstration of Swift's ingenious capacity to adapt almost anything to the attack on Wood (such as the title of Wycherley's play, *Love in a Wood*). Thus, instead of selecting and ordering details so as to construct a form which acts as a defense against multiplicity, Swift appears to embrace that multiplicity, seeking to immerse himself in an infinite variety of particulars that are only marginally or accidentally related to one another.[14]

England correctly recognizes the plethora of tactics Swift brings to bear on Wood, but what he does not see is that the random acts of satiric violence Swift seems to embrace "fortuitously" can coherently, even "thematically," structure the last half of the poem by linking Wood's political downfall with his sodomization. Beginning at the point where Swift's narrator tells us about the false saint and Wood's wimbled bum ("I ne'er could endure my talent to smother, / I told you one tale, I will tell you another" [69–70]), the "miscellaneous" images of sodomization, victimization, and execution all fit into a narrative sequence in which Swift strategically exploits the discourse of sodomy to figure Wood both as homosexual victim and agent in an inexorable progression from one identity to the other.

We have already seen above how Swift uses sodomy as a hermeneutic method for finding out the truth about Wood. By proposing that the Irish "bore him behind" and "wimble his bum," (78–79) Swift's narrator gives us a proleptic demonstration of Wood's true nature:

> I'll hold you a groat, when you wimble his bum,
> He'll bellow as loud as a de'il in a drum:
>
> (79–80)

Wood will "bellow" like a devil and thus distinguish himself from the false saint that "makes no complaint" when the good Irish joiner bores its breech. It is impossible to tell from Swift's poem if Wood would bellow in pain or in pleasure, but the important point is that both false "saint" and true "devil" may be distinguished both from each other and from other "men" through sodomy. The joiner's phallic auger, when turned on the British coiner, elicits Wood's devilishness in the same way it reveals the falseness of an "image" that perversely acquiesces in an act that here has ramifications *only* for the "passive" or "receptive" partner. Swift's addressees escape the stigma of becoming sodomites in their own right because their aggression toward Wood is only political and meant to display his social unworthiness. Their political activity places them in the same category with Trumbach's masculine rake whose sodomitical association with other boys and men, while threatening political and religious norms, only reinforces his masculine identity. After, for instance, describing the sexual prerogatives of Restoration libertines, Trumbach concludes that

> The unconventionality of that minority of rakes who were sodomitical was therefore frightening to society at large; *but they were not held in contempt.* It was, instead, that they were secretly held in awe for the extremity of their masculine self-assertion, since they triumphed over male and female alike.[15]

Just as the libertine becomes more masculine because of his male appetite for both male and female bodies, so Swift's male joiner, the presumptive male narrator of Swift's poem, and the putative male addressee of Swift's satire become more political, and perhaps even more politically correct, by partaking in Wood's sodomization. For Wood and his tormentors, male sexual identity collapses into political identity, so that to speak of buggering Wood as a sexual act would be, at least for the characters in Swift's poem, to miss the point of Swift's argument entirely. Refiguring Wood's trial by auger as an abominable exercise in homosexual penetration would not, I argue, lessen Swift's rhetorical investment evident in Wood's ordeal, since the same-sex associations Swift conjures up in Wood's fantasized sodomization exist only as communal associations guaranteeing both the perpetuation and reinforcement of Ireland's political autonomy.

Political identity in this case becomes the rationale for whatever male same-sex association proves necessary to prevent Wood's successful "arrival" (75) in Ireland. Swift's narrator eagerly accedes to Wood's rape as a device for creating the common "you" of his audience:

> From me I declare you shall have no denial,
> And there can be no harm in making a trial;
> And when to the joy of your hearts he has roared,
> You may show him about for a new groaning board.
>
> (81–84)

"Showing" Wood's penetrated body about as the community's "new groaning board" is a requisite part of creating this new male and political bond, of moving from the "you" who shall not be denied to the plural "you" whose hearts joy to hear Wood roar. The spectacle of Wood's body, suspended upon and controlled by a phallic Irish bore, now displays his true relation to the community of Irish patriots who have mastered him: he is not part of the community, but his visible presence as object of the community's sodomizing political intent continually refers back to that community in a powerfully reintegrating gesture.

Wood's sodomization explains how Swift can meaningfully pun on the titles of Etherege's play, *Love in a Tub*, and Wycherley's play, *Love in a Wood*. The surface tension between Wood's name and Wycherley's play sets up Swift's trope, but the imagery of sodomy that has to this point shaped Wood's encounter with the Irish insures that the trope itself continues to coordinate sodomy with Wood's political downfall. Swift explains the love Wood has for us as *Love in a Tub* and then shows us how this false love becomes *Love in a Wood*:

> First, *Love in a Tub*: 'squire Wood has in store
> Strong tubs for his raps, two thousand and more;
> These raps he will honestly dig out with shovels,
> And sell them for gold, or he can't show his love else.

> Wood swears he will do it for Ireland's good,
> Then can you deny it is *Love in a Wood*?
>
> (95–100)

There is a certain satiric distance between how Wood would love us and how we will love Wood. Wood shows his esteem for the Irish people by disseminating "raps," or debased copper halfpence, throughout Ireland. His love thus has real consequences for those Irishmen who mistake it for a worthwhile investment in themselves and in their country, since Ireland's economy will be inundated with such counterfeit tokens of affection:

> For when to express a friend's love we are willing,
> We never say more than, your love is a million;
> But with honest Wood's love there is no contending,
> 'Tis fifty round millions of love, and a mending.
>
> (103–6)

Swift distinguishes between friendly love and Wood's love by counterbalancing the relationship between friends with Wood's duplicity: predictably, the balance fails. To compensate for this failure, it becomes necessary to return Wood's "love" in suitable kind. By sodomizing Wood, by literalizing Wycherley's title and impaling Wood's anus on an Irish auger, Swift returns Wood's love in a fitting manner and allows Irish patriots a chance to experience *Love in a Wood*, at least from Wood's anus on.

Swift's scenario for Wood closes with one last story from the poem's narrator:

> Hear one story more, and then I will stop.
> I dreamt Wood was told he should die by a drop:
> So methought, he resolved no liquor to taste,
> For fear the first drop might as well be his last:

> But dreams are like oracles, hard to explain 'em,
> For it proved that he died of a drop at Kilmainham:
> I waked with delight, and not without hope,
> Very soon to see Wood drop down from a rope.
>
> (109–16)

Wood ends his life on the gallows at Kilmainham, as a proper English sodomite should.[16] As a sodomite, Wood suffers at both ends of the crime. First, he is sodomitically "de-manned" as a potential member of Ireland's political fraternity, becoming nothing more than a "groaning board" for Swift's puns. Then he meets the capital end reserved for such as himself who, however unwillingly, experience the prohibited physicality among men that, increasingly in the eighteenth century, defines Wood's crime against England's Irishmen. His misreading of his own end helps make him, certainly, an appropriate dupe for Swift's comedy, but it also helps to obscure the sodomitical narrative of perverse sexuality and capital punishment into which Wood's narrative may be rendered. Much of the sexual violence in "A Serious Poem" depends upon an unstated expectation that Wood's masculinity be vulnerable to Swift's sodomitical manipulations. Wood must be recognizably male so that he may be degraded from the masculine identity he might otherwise share with those in the political community, so that the character who bellows "like a de'il in a drum" when he is penetrated does not willingly take part in the act or complicate sodomy's exclusionary deployment by expressing an uncomfortably reciprocal interest in those assaulting him. Swift's satire on Wood works at its most basic level by distancing Wood from any point of commonality with his persecutors, and while there is nothing new with allying satire and the politics of exclusion, there is also evidently nothing new with effecting that exclusion via sodomy.

To pursue the politics of exclusion even further, Swift sometimes transposes sodomitical imagery from one symbolic register to another as part of a larger political attack. We can see this sort of strategic formulation of sodomy in Swift's poem, "Mad Mullinix and Timothy," the first of a series of political satires directed against Richard Tighe, a Whig member of the Irish parliament and a particular enemy of Swift's.[17] "Mad Mullinix and Timothy," which first appeared in 1728, takes the form of a dialogue between Tighe, or "Timothy," and Mullinix, "a half-crazed beggar who went round Dublin spouting Tory sentiments."[18] Swift inverts the relationship between this "half-crazed beggar" and the supposedly sane Tighe by having "mad" Mullinix admonish Timothy for his own bursts of outrage:

> M. I own 'tis not my bread and butter,
> But prithee Tim, why all this clutter?
> Why ever in these raging fits,
> Damning to hell the Jacobits?
> When, if you search the kingdom round,
> There's hardly twenty to be found;
> No, not among the priests and friars.
>
> (1–7)

In this first verse paragraph, Mullinix establishes Timothy's excessive political zeal against adherents of the deposed James II's family as a symptom of Timothy's own madness. Timothy responds to Mullinix's rebuke with characteristic Whig zeal simply by ignoring the proposition of Mullinix's statement that "'Twixt you and me God damns the liars" (8). Mullinix and Timothy then engage in an exchange of under- and overstatements about the Tories and their putative devotion to George I and the house of Hanover, and about the earl of Barrymore's call for an investigation into the administration of Ireland's public accounts, especially as fraudulently administered by John Pratt, the deputy vice-treasurer:[19]

M. The Tories are gone every man over
To our illustrious house of Hanover.
From all their conduct this is plain,
And then—T. God damn the liars again.
Did not an earl but lately vote
To bring in (I could cut his throat)
Our whole account of public debts?
M. Lord how this frothy coxcomb frets! [*aside*]
T. Did not an able statesman bishop
This dangerous horrid motion dish up?
As Popish craft? Did he not rail on't?
Show fire and faggot in the tail on't?
Proving the earl a grand offender,
And in a plot for the Pretender?
Whose fleet, in all our friends' opinion,
Was then embarking at Avignon.

(9–24)

As pertinent as these topical political references are to understanding
Timothy's character, the next few lines, which Rogers omits from
his edition of the poem and reprints only in the explanatory notes,
give us Timothy's true political character and method of political inquiry:

M. In every arse you run your snout,
To find this damned Pretender out,
While all the silly wretch can do,
Is but to frisk about like you.
But Tim, convinced by your persuasion,
I yield there might be an invasion,
And you who never fart in vain,
Can fart his navy back again.

T. Zounds, sir. M. But to be short and serious
For long disputes will only weary us.

(24–25)[20]

Timothy obscenely and sodomitically penetrates every ass to sniff
out Jacobitism in what will be the first of a series of images in
which Swift conflates Timothy's political suspicion of "Jacobits"
and his unfortunate tendency towards sodomitical penetration.
Sodomy serves here as a failed hermeneutic device for finding out
both the Pretender, James Edward, and his supporters, in that Timothy never finds what he looks for, but the lines leave us with an
importantly ambiguous reading. Construed one way, the Pretender
to England's throne becomes a "silly wretch," who, like Timothy,
"frisks about" imposing his perverse attentions on the asses of an
unresponsive and hostile audience. Construed another way, these
lines about "the silly wretch" whose only possible option "Is but to
frisk about like you" simultaneously categorize and indict as
sodomitically perverse and politically impotent anyone from the
Pretender down who shares Timothy's opinions.

Such images of sodomitical imposition recur throughout the
poem. How, for instance, should we interpret Mullinix's reference
to Timothy's malcontent insinuations?

Thy peevish, and perpetual teasing,
With plots; and Jacobites and treason;
Thy busy never-meaning face;
Thy screwed-up front; thy state grimace;
Thy formal nods; important sneers;
Thy whisperings foisted in all ears;
(Which are, whatever you may think,
But nonsense wrapped up in a stink)
Have made thy presence in a true sense

> To thy own side so damned a nuisance,
> That when they have you in their eye,
> As if the devil drove, they fly.
>
> (47–58)

The "peevish, and perpetual teasing / With plots; and Jacobites and treason" that becomes Timothy's "whisperings foisted in all ears" is a more successful inversion of Timothy's original sodomitical hermeneutic, because these unwanted and annoying intrusions into the bodies and body politic of Timothy's compatriots convey to them the truth of his madness as "nonsense wrapped up in a stink." If, after all, to "foist" is "to introduce surreptitiously or unwarrantably into" (OED), then the vehicle for Timothy's political subversion is a metaphor of physical penetration whereby Timothy violates the presumptive male body of Irish politics. The image of "foisted whisperings" itself constitutes both an extension and an elaboration of Timothy's intrusive, arse-sniffing snout. Timothy's nose up every ass becomes his whisperings in all ears, insofar as both images register his continued and detestable contact with Ireland's political community.

Mullinix's long comparison between Timothy and Punchinello makes this point even clearer. When Timothy swears that

> And while this vital breath I blow,
> Or from above, or from below,
> I'll sputter, swagger, curse and rail,
> The Tories' terror, scourge and flail.
>
> (73–76)

Mullinix reveals that Timothy's true value to the Tories lies in his acting just as he does:

> M. Tim, you mistake the matter quite,
> The Tories! you are their delight.

> And should you act a different part,
> Be grave and wise, 'twould break their heart.
> Why, Tim, you have a taste I know,
> And often see a puppet-show.
> Observe, the audience is in pain,
> While Punch is hid behind the scene,
> But when they hear his rusty voice,
> With what impatience they rejoice.
>
> (77–86)

As much as this scene depends upon the language of puppetry and theater, it also depends upon the obscene sexuality associated with Punchinello, who assimilates Timothy's nosey, ass-poking transgression in the figure of his own "monstrously" phallic nose:

> If Punch, to spur their fancy, shows
> In at the door his monstrous nose,
> Then sudden draws it back again,
> O what a pleasure mixed with pain!
> You every moment think an age,
> Till he appears upon the stage.
>
> (93–98)

Timothy/Punch puts his nose in and out of puppet-theater politics much as Timothy puts *his* nose in and out of Irish fundaments, only now his action produces a perverse "pleasure mixed with pain" corresponding directly to the Tory pleasure in Timothy's Whig idiocy. This is the same Punch who

> Reviles all people in his jargon,
> And sells the King of Spain a bargain.
> St George himself he plays the wag on,
> And mounts astride upon the dragon.

> He gets a thousand thumps and kicks
> Yet cannot leave his roguish tricks;
> In every action thrusts his nose
> The reason why no mortal knows.
>
> (103–10)

Timothy/Punch's freedom derives not only from the transgressive license he takes with authority, but also from the delighted ease with which his audience consumes his inexplicable incursions into the social order around him. He can make a fool of the king of Spain or ride St. George's dragon, and while his pranks earn him "a thousand thumps and kicks," the audience watches eagerly on to see how he "In every action thrusts his nose / The reason why no mortal knows."

Punch's phallic noses pleases, even when it "thrusts" incomprehensibly in where it has, and can have, no reason to be. Indeed, that is its very attraction for those who, like Swift, gain pleasure from this puppet show of Irish politics.[21] They neither do nor wish to do what Punch does, but watching his "teasing" supplies its own gratification in a manner that cannot be divorced from the voyeuristic and sexual:

> While teasing all, by all he's teased,
> How well are the spectators pleased!
> Who in the motion have no share;
> But purely come to hear, and stare;
>
> (115–18)

It is enough to see Punch and his nose at work doing whatever he pleases; he has thumps and kicks enough for punishment, and his actions give form to an otherwise inarticulable desire that reason and the law prohibit, and that expresses, and becomes expressible as, a risible political sentiment.

Swift's Punch figure is not a traditional symbol of homosexual sodomy, but its concatenation with other images associated with a perverse male body makes this scene read as if the "pleasure mixed with pain" that Punch inspires were a sodomitical pleasure integrating Timothy/Punch in the potential for homosexual, penetrative contact. This concatenation places Timothy/Punch in close proximity to images of the discourse of sodomy with which we are already familiar. Just as his nose penetrates "in at the door" and leaves "a pleasure mixed with pain" when he "sudden draws it back again," so the penetration of "things in things" works in sodomy to provide access both to illicit sodomitical pleasures and to the epistemological status of sodomitical acts. Timothy/Punch's proximity to figures available to the discourse of sodomy is itself a refiguring of that discourse as political and therefore appropriate to Tighe, who thus becomes a fit and recognizable object of Swift's aggression by way of this sodomitical association.

The same formulation of political identity through sodomy happens to John, Lord Hervey in "Bounce to Fop," a poem first published in 1736 and variously attributed to Swift, Pope, and Gay.[22] Styled "An Heroic Epistle from a Dog at Twickenham to a Dog at Court," "Bounce to Fop" recounts the differences between Bounce, Pope's plain country bitch, and Fop, a courtly lapdog perhaps owned by Henrietta Howard, countess of Suffolk. "Bounce to Fop" stresses Bounce's unaffected country nature and contrasts her wholesome "nobility" to the conniving sexual and political intrigues of Fop's court existence:

> Fop! you can dance and make a leg,
> Can fetch and carry, cringe and beg,
> And (what's the top of all your tricks)
> Can stoop to pick up *strings* and *sticks*.
> We country dogs love nobler sport,
> And scorn the pranks of dogs at court.

> Fie, naughty Fop! where e'er you come
> To fart and piss about the room,
> To lay your head in every lap,
> And, when they think not of you, snap!
> The worst that envy, or that spite
> E'er said of me, is, I can bite:
> That sturdy vagrants, rogues in rags,
> Who poke at me, can make no brags;
> And that to touse such things as *flutter*,
> To honest Bounce is bread and butter.

(9–24)

This passage establishes the political atmosphere of court life as "honest Bounce" sees it. Fop's attentions seem consistent with what one might innocently expect from a courtly spaniel who is free to lay its head in every lap, but implicit in the image is a juxtaposition of mouth and genitals that underwrites the permissibility of Fop's fawning and "snapping." Fop has access, however veiled, to both male and female "laps," so that the possibility of perverse sexual contact foreign to "country dogs" like Bounce here pervades "court dog" imagery and opens space for the perverse reading of court society.

Bounce, on the other hand, prides herself on her invulnerability to such contact, since her claim is "That sturdy vagrants, rogues in rags, / Who poke at me, can make no brags, / And that to touse [tear] such things as *flutter* / To honest Bounce is bread and butter." Bounce's superiority to the artifice of court allows her to sense the truth about court life, though, as with Fop, she too delves under the cover of sumptuously arrayed laps:

> While you, and every courtly fop,
> Fawn on the devil for a chop,
> I've the humanity to hate

A butcher, though he brings me meat;
And let me tell you, have a nose,
(Whatever stinking fops suppose)
That under cloth of gold or tissue,
Can smell a plaster, or an issue.

                                                    (25–32)

Like Fop, Bounce encounters the Hanoverian court's hidden side, but unlike Fop's sexualized relationship with "every lap," Bounce's nose ostensibly goes under "cloth of gold or tissue" only to sniff out the truth of a concealed "plaster, or an issue" specific to the sexual decadence of court existence. With courtly perversity established, Swift (probably with Pope's editorial assistance) assigns Hervey to the rank of these scheming court dogs who typically attain their own political goals through perverse sexual titillation, and whose diseased end Bounce triumphantly announces:

When all such dogs have had their days,
As knavish Pams and fawning Trays;
When pampered Cupids, beastly Veni's,
And motley, squinting Harvequini's,
Shall lick no more their lady's breech,
But die of looseness, claps, or itch;
Fair Thames from either echoing shore
Shall hear, and dread my manly roar.

                                                    (37–44)

Rogers identifies the Harvequini figure with Lord Hervey, and if the identification holds, it is because of the sodomitical stimulation of my lady's "breech," or anus, typifying Hervey's marginalized sexuality.[23] Jill Campbell has written how such eighteenth-century writers as Pope, Fielding, and William Pulteney stressed Hervey's bi- or homosexuality as a dominant factor in his political identity:

Over and over again, these writers focus on Hervey as a representative of the corruption of Walpole's ministry, and over and over again they, like Pulteney, suggest a connection between Hervey's sexual ambiguities and the ethical ambiguities of his political associations.[24]

Nowhere in Swift's (or Swift's and Pope's) poem is this elision of sexual identity by political identity more evident than in the lines about the deaths of fawning court dogs who live to lick their mistresses' "breeches." Swift here replaces the transgressive freedom and energy that distinguished Timothy/Punch's sodomitical incursions in "Mad Mullinix and Timothy" with images of diseased "looseness, claps, or itch" that put an end to the courtly and debased sodomy of aristocratic analingus, and consequently, an end to the system of patronage and sexual reward that characterizes Hervey's life.

The identity to which Hervey is assigned is thus one that "has its day" in a temporal succession where the "honest," those who have "the humanity to hate," always outlive their perverse rivals and accede to a natural position of political influence. It is Bounce, after all, who is guaranteed a posterity: Fop's generation of sodomitical court "dogs" passes away and leaves Bounce and her brood victoriously in its place, for once Fop's effeminate "lady-lap-dogship" (6) dies, "Fair Thames from either echoing shore / Shall hear, and dread [Bounce's] manly roar" (43–44):

> See Bounce, like Berecynthia, crowned
> With thundering offspring all around,
> Beneath, beside me, and atop,
> A hundred sons! and not one Fop.
>
> (45–48)

Bounce's "manly roar" couples with her own prodigious fertility to eradicate all strains of politically suspect identities like Hervey's, so that the effeminate and sodomitical "court dog" ceases to be a factor in English government. Such "manliness" in a female figure may seem strange and even counterproductive, given the ideological difference Swift is attempting to install, but in this poem at least, Bounce's manliness marks the strict alliance of both the power of heterosexual reproduction and of the heterosexually gendered identities directing that power, and it explains how "life" comes to be rigorously associated with Bounce's natural heterosexuality and "death" with Hervey's foppish perversity. Bounce's manliness insures that among her hundred sons there will be "not one Fop," and that the likes of sodomites as Hervey really will have ceased to be a problem, while her regal (re)productivity preserves the proper sexual distinction between male and female.

The conceit of Swift's poem may seem a witty treatment of inconsequentials, but its light satire makes it all the easier for the poem to encode a persistent and normalizing Western fantasy that once all of the sodomites like Hervey have died off, the world will be a permanently better place. Bounce's heterosexual fertility gives her and her kind life beyond Fop's death and allows her the leisure to establish a proper and heterosexually mandated political regime. Indeed, "life" is so strongly linked to Bounce's fantasy of political succession that in it she lives on even after death, because once the regime is in place,

> Then Bounce ('tis all that Bounce can crave)
> Shall wag her tail within the grave.
>
> (81–82)

The fantasy does not, of course, work, as even Bounce tacitly admits when she prays:

> And O! would fate the bliss decree
> To mine (a bliss too great for me)

That two, my tallest sons, might grace
Attending each with stately pace,
Iülus' side, as erst Evander's,
To keep off flatterers, spies, and panders,
To let no noble slave come near,
And *scare Lord Fannies from his ear*
Then might a royal youth, and true,
Enjoy at least a friend—or two:
A treasure, which, of royal kind,
Few but himself deserve to find.

(69–80; emphasis added)

Are Bounce's sons to scare persistent Lord Fannies from Iülus's ear, or rear? It makes little difference since, as we have seen, both sites may be sodomitically suborned by homosexual politicians. What remains important here is that fops like Hervey will at some future date no longer trouble England's political order with their unnatural sexuality. Bounce's sons insure that Iülus's "friend or two" are not also sexual partners bent on stimulating the heir's ear or his anus unduly. This sort of policed social contact between the Prince of Wales and his friends introduces the possibility of a homosocial, but importantly nonsexual, association that could replace the Walpolean all-male and suspect government with which Hervey's troublesome homosexuality has come to be identified. Campbell writes,

Walpole's leadership accelerated England's movement, begun in 1688, from a government focused upon the theatrical image of a royal *family* to a government dominated by a prime minister and his network of faithful male agents and place-holders. Some of the most characteristic themes both of opposition satire and of its political theorizing express resistance to this change—from the popular complaint that

the structure of the royal family has been turned inside out
by Caroline's domination of George, and by Walpole's domination of her . . . to the grotesque representations of the
new style of government as a male club, held together by
the exchange of dirty money and flattery and by acts of
abjection to Walpole's broad rear-end.[25]

Bounce's vision of England draws heavily on the older images of
good government in which natural, heterosexual families protect
England's political institutions and perpetuate the tradition of heterosexual rule. Hervey's interests, like Fop's, have no place in this tradition because these interests persistently introduce an unnatural,
unproductive sexuality into English politics where it perniciously
replaces fertility with perversity and death. Hervey's bodily politics
are unalterably different from the "nobler sport" Bounce loves because, instead of producing the "thundering offspring" needed to govern England, Hervey spends his sexual and political (sexual *become*
political) energies licking breeches and machinating for Walpole.
Within the mutual parameters "Bounce to Fop" sets for male sexuality and political empowerment, Hervey remains unrecoverable.

This sodomitically determined sort of male identity, one that
invests the anus with an unnatural and unnaturalizable value, is
itself capable of reincorporating the excremental anality that has
so influenced the interpretive history of Swift's scatological poems.
In "Clad all in Brown" (published 1745), for instance, the figure of
Richard Tighe reroutes images of degraded female sexuality through
an anally determined male sexuality to condense Tighe's political
identity.[26] Characteristically, Tighe's anal sexuality exceeds even female depravity, and it is precisely because this perverse anal excess
supersedes and assimilates the poem's examples of depraved femininity that Tighe's character becomes so abominable. The poem, a
parody of Cowley's "Clad All in White,"[27] begins by asking why
"Dick" (Tighe) looks the way he does:

Foulest brute that stinks below,
Why in this brown doest thou appear?

(1–2)

Without stopping to answer its own rhetoric, the poem describes Dick as able to exceed his own already superlative foulness:

For, wouldst thou make a fouler show,
Thou must go naked all the year,
Fresh from the mud a wallowing sow
Would then be not so brown as thou.

(3–6)

Significantly, the image against which Dick's shitty excess appears is one of bestial femaleness. The "wallowing sow's" unmediated access to mud, undesirable in itself, is preferable to Dick's excremental exterior, and the sow's presumptively natural affinity for dirt sets off Dick's perverse character by showing (1) how very foul Dick is now and (2) how foul he can become. Physically, there is little difference between Dick naked or Dick clothed:

'Tis not the coat that looks so dun,
His hide emits a foulness out,
Not one jot better looks the sun
Seen from behind a dirty clout:
So turds within a glass enclose,
The glass will seem as brown as those.

(7–12)

In fact, the simile between Dick's clothes and a glass enclosing turds is calculated to fail: just as Dick's clothes seem brown because they enclose him, so the glass seems brown because it encases shit, but the relationship, typically, exceeds the terms of the figure. Unlike the turds that the glass effectively contains, the "foulness" "his hide emits" contaminates its surroundings so that even if his coat could be separated from Dick's filth itself, it still could not contain him:

> Thou now one heap of foulness art,
> All outward and within is foul;
> Condenséd filth in every part,
> Thy body's clothéd like thy soul.
> Thy soul, which through thy hide of buff,
> Scarce glimmers, like a dying snuff.
>
> (13–18)

At this point, the link between Dick's moral character and his physical sexuality is less important than the images of excess that establish that character, but it becomes increasingly difficult to maintain a separation between moral and sexual states as the poem proceeds.

Swift's next move, for example, is to channel Dick's filthiness through the marginal sexuality of female prostitutes, or "bawds." Swift constitutes these bawds by means of a double simile between themselves and Dick:

> Old carted bawds such garments wear,
> When pelted all with dirt they shine;
> Such their *exalted* bodies are,
> As shrivelled and as black as thine.
>
> (19–22)

Dick's clothes are *like* those of the bawds, his excremental body is *like* their "shrivelled and black" carcasses. But by reversing the similes thus, we can see how Dick's foul body actually underwrites Swift's surface comparison by which the meaning of the bawds' bodies would be conferred on Dick's. The bawds may seem equally as base as Dick, but it is with his body that meaningful categories of sexual denigration originate, since he is the point to which Swift's comparison refers for its notion of degree. Associating Dick with a debased female sexuality such as prostitution is, consequently, only a secondary maneuver meant to emphasize the inverted gender hierarchy that here gives male and female sexual identities their relative worth. Bawds, that is, are bad, but no bawd is as bad as the dickly Tighe. If we were to substitute Dick's sexually depraved body for those of the "old carted bawds," we would see by how much he surpasses them:

> If thou wert in a cart, I fear
> Thou wouldst be pelted worse than they're.
>
> (23–24)

Swift, in other words, rewrites female sexuality as a component of male anality and then subsumes both constructs in Dick's political identity:

> Yet when we see thee thus arrayed,
> The neighbours think it is but just
> That thou shouldst take an honest trade,
> And weekly carry out our dust.
>
> (25–28)

Dick's excremental raiment, the synecdochic extension of his all-embrowning anus, appropriates the opprobrium of female prostitution and fits him to take up an "honest trade" as shit collector (as opposed to his dishonest Whig career of making trouble for good Tories like Swift).

But the most important relation between Dick and the carted bawds is one impacted in the identity-conferring simile itself. If Dick's anally defined body is truly "Such [as] their *exalted* bodies are," then he too becomes the used-up relic of male sexual attention. The bodies of old female prostitutes are worn-out sites of sexual exchange with men, sites of penetration where the ravages of intercourse for money take their toll on increasingly "shrivelled and black" female forms. If Dick is as like these forms as the simile suggests, the excremental anality that defines his perversion is in its own turn structured by an encrypted sodomitical principle of same-sex contact that governs the hostile rhetoric of Swift's poem. Sodomy as a poetic strategy is possible because Swift utilizes the bawds' subordinated female sexuality as part of Dick's totalizing masculine perversion, which bears the brunt of Swift's political critique. But that perverse masculinity itself finally displaces the prostitutes from their position on the margin of society and forces them back upon polite culture as a more acceptable alternative than the sodomitical one Dick presents. Dick's sodomitical male identity finally allows his identification by and with his own anus and then, in the poem's last couplet, transforms him into that anus:

> Of cleanly houses who will doubt,
> When Dick cries, "Dust to carry out"?
>
> (29–30)

Dick becomes the sodomized anus that carries out "our dust" from Swift's body politic, and, in its own turn, that anus becomes an appropriate means of making houses "cleanly" because of its sodomitical subordination to the political order. Sodomy insures the social order of this poem even as it erodes the difference between Dick and his female constituents, since their mutually ostracized sexuality renders them expendable satiric targets for the aggression of a well-regulated neighborhood of "cleanly houses" made pure by their filth.

To interpret Swift's sodomitical poetry, we need to understand how thoroughly sodomy as a discursive practice can come to pervade all types of Swiftian discourse about the body in its relation to culture, whether that relation is physiological, medical, legal, religious, sexual, or economic. By way of sodomy all of these relations can be refigured as political and therefore subject to intervention. The discourse of sodomy as Swift uses it is expansive enough to contain differences in class (as Tighe the member of Parliament finds out when Swift allies him with Dublin's prostitutes and madmen), in sexuality (as the effeminate Fop discovers when vanquished by Bounce's heroic sexuality), in gender (as Wood discovers when Swift's hardy and hard Irishmen sodomitically best him without themselves being bested), even in ontology (as Gulliver's uncertain grasp of the "natural" makes clear). In some cases, most notably Wood's, sodomy reiterates a gender difference that inheres despite Wood's sexual similarity to his rapists, so that the nonnecessity of "natural" gendered identity appears against the sodomitically violent, even homophobic background of that very same identity.

Swift's poems, in short, show just how images of perverse and prohibited sexuality either relate to and grow out of a core image of sodomy, as in "Mad Mullinix and Timothy" or "A Serious Poem Upon William Wood," or how such perverse sexualities transpose the category of sodomy from the realm of acts to the realm of being, as with "Clad All in Brown." Political analogues of sodomy like Wood's "wimbling," Tighe/Timothy's zealous "sniffing," or Fop's "snapping"—which everyone can read safely as sexually neutral satire only by ignoring the violence of Swift's images—suddenly appropriate the rhetorical power of sodomy itself when the wit of satire wears thin and the violent reorganization of identity becomes a political possibility Swift's satires can enact. The figure of the sodomite is a richly transformative one affording Swift articulations of class, gender, sexuality, and ethnicity that redefine the political dynamic in which he wishes to intervene, and that, without the discourse of sodomy, are lost to him. But always underlying this political expedience is the violence of sodomy, a cultural violence that Swift can exploit because it is ingrained in any possible manifestation of the term.

THREE

Pope's *To Cobham* and *To a Lady:* Empiricism and the Synecdochic Woman

Readings of Alexander Pope's paired epistles on male and female character, *To Cobham* and *To a Lady*,[1] have usually emphasized these poems' generic continuity with, and sometimes manipulation of, a history of writings on character shaped by Theophrastan notions of the "character" as genre and by the essays of Montaigne.[2] Pope's use of this tradition often stresses the character sketch as a means of juxtaposing two different but related orders of activity: the individual sketched comes more closely to resemble a type represented in the character just as the type or image presented by the character takes on a certain epistemological concreteness through its individuation.[3] Further, the Popean character sketch often describes an individual's inconsistency while using the occasion of the sketch to generate a principle of epistemological stability out of the apparent disorder inherent in individual personalities.[4]

Considering Pope's character sketches as examples of a genre should, theoretically, allow us to argue that the categorical preconditions for establishing criteria of character remain the same from poem to poem. Benjamin Boyce, for example, gives the following generic configuration for a character, which, since it is generic, would presumably apply to any character, regardless of sex:

> The Character as Theophrastus created it is a picture of an imaginary person who represents the group of men possessed by that feature of character . . . which dominates him. He is to be imagined as alive and individual; but because he is to be seen only in those situations that reveal his dominant moral or psychological habit, the picture will be eclectic, the shadowing heightened. . . . He represents a large group of men, ancient and modern, and so, in a sense, is not an exaggeration of human nature. But the picture by shadowing will exaggerate him. The figures depicted in Theophrastus' Characters, with one or two exceptions, are not theoretical but real; in all cases they are types.[5]

Boyce's definition of character illustrates the problem I will examine in this chapter, since its significance lies in what Boycean character does and does not include: Boyce's Theophrastan character is defined by a series of observable actions ("those situations that reveal his dominant moral or psychological habit") that reflect some unchanging trait of the individuals examined. The principle of accurate observability underlying these actions is itself never in question because to doubt the accuracy of those observations providing us with a picture of character would be, according to the terms of Boyce's argument, to do away with the possibility of a generic character sketch at all. Even the element of fantasy that goes into the character's composition ("he is imagined to be alive and individual") is, in an important sense, simply a refraction of an ultimately observable reality. In other words, the poem's correspondence with the empirically valid at some level guarantees both the individual sketch and the genre as a whole.

What gets left out of Boyce's explanation, of course, is an explicit consciousness that women as well as men really exist and can be observed in the same way.[6] Boyce's definition of character apparently describes a stable methodology for recognizing whatever individual traits abstract neatly to the general level of character; this methodology of observation would thus seem equally applicable to men and women. But Boyce's method, like much of the poetry it refers to, obscures questions of sexuality, and specifically of sexual difference, simply by omitting women from its considerations entirely. Sexual difference as a criterion for determining generic status thus disappears from Boyce's method, and as a consequence his method has no way to tell whether or not sexual difference establishes a generic difference between male and female characters. Like Boyce, Pope excludes women at critical moments in the process of establishing character while at the same time constructing different gendered identities according to similar generic imperatives. Sexual difference is ostensibly the justification for those generic distinctions between the sexes that Pope describes in his epistles, but as I will maintain, sexual difference does not make enough of a *formal* difference to support the claims Pope uses it to enforce. Pope's epistolary characters agree both in principle and in detail with many of Boyce's strictures, and much of the criticism surrounding *To Cobham* and *To a Lady* has been informed by the method Boyce describes.[7] But by eliding the theoretical complications that a principle of sexual difference entails, Pope allows the category of "sexuality" to stand in for other, less obviously sexual differences in class and political standing, while by overdetermining the same category, critics of Pope's poetry allow sexuality a theoretical difference just as difficult to sustain.

Bishop Warburton, for example, uses the underlying exemplarity of male and female characters as a way to prove the two epistles' generic coherence when taken together. Warburton writes that readers who expect both epistles to work exactly the same way miss the larger view of gendered character the epistles provide:

The reader, perhaps, may be disappointed to find that this *epistle* [*To a Lady*], which proposes the same subject with the preceding [*To Cobham*], is conducted on very different rules of composition; for instead of being disposed in the same logical method, and filled with the like philosophical remarks, it is wholly taken up in drawing a great variety of capital characters: But if he would reflect, that the *two Sexes* make but *one Species*, and consequently, that the characters of both must be studied and explained on the same principles, he would see, that when the Poet had done this in the preceding epistles, his business here was, not to repeat what he had already delivered, but only to verify and illustrate his doctrine, by every *view* of that perplexity of Nature, which *his* Philosophy only can explain.[8]

Warburton gives us a synergistic view of the sexual components of human character. According to Warburton, Pope uses the same general method to study the two sexually distinct types of identity because "the characters of both must be studied and explained on the same principles." Warburton thus identifies an overarching Popean methodology like the one Boyce proposes, in that both Pope and Boyce base the character sketch as a genre on similarly observable particulars. Indeed, Warburton implicitly claims that Pope goes farther than Boyce, since Pope "studies" and "explains" male *and* female character according to "the same principles." If Pope thus seems to "conduct" *To a Lady* "on very different rules of composition" from those of *To Cobham*, it is only because the same explanatory principles dictate a differing form of expression for each of the two sexes. Warburton goes on to tell us that the extraordinary thing about Pope's accomplishment in *To a Lady* "is, that all the great strokes in the several characters of *Women* are not only infinitely perplexed and discordant, like those in *Men*, but absolutely inconsistent, and in a much higher degree contradictory."

The really telling point, though, is that "As strange as this may appear, yet [the reader] will see that the Poet has all the while strictly followed Nature . . ." (363). For Warburton, while sexual differences yield different characters, one philosophical approach suffices to explain these differences as congruent parts of the same general Nature, so that much of the potential difference between men and women is recuperated as an issue of observable degree. Women, after all, may be just as "infinitely perplexed and discordant" as men, and if "infinite perplexity and discord" with one's self may be read as "contradiction," women remain like men, only "in a much higher degree." Consequently, much of what we can read as sexual difference in Warburton is for him more a matter of sexual congruence.

Warburton's secondhand misogyny is thus an effect of the referential proof he finds in Pope's texts and calls on to support his own reading. Genre's relation to gender is especially clear here, as Warburton shows by making Pope's epistle on male character the model of a philosophical method for which *To a Lady* will then act as the exemplary proof that "verifies and illustrates [Pope's] doctrine." Masculinity's "philosophical" character as displayed by the male epistle thus becomes an appropriate counterpart to the "exemplarity" of feminine character in the female epistle. In each case, the sketch adequately represents the truth of male and female reality by "strictly following Nature, whose ways we find . . . are not a little mysterious; and a mystery this might have remained, had not our Author explained it . . ." (363). For Warburton, the generic complementarity of the two texts is simply a sign of their deeper fidelity to the identity of and relation between the sexes. Associating *To Cobham* with the philosophical substance of character, and *To a Lady* with its empirical expression, is itself an example of Pope's genius for fitting a generic form to its proper poetic subject, and just as "gender" and "character" come together to form a distinctive genre, so "male" and "female" come together to form Warburton's notion of "*one Species.*"

But, as the critical history of these two poems continues to show, arguments over the epistemological foundation of gender and its possible representation in the *Epistles* have tended to polarize around sexual difference and its accessibility to Pope's epistemological claims. Both *To Cobham* and *To a Lady* generate ideas of masculinity and femininity based on categorical statements about men and woman and what gendered subjects can be and do in the society Pope represents, but the relation between male and female characters in these texts also sparks questions about the differences between the sexes and about the kinds of knowledge establishing each sex in its own right as a conceptual category. Laura Brown's work on the connection between generic form and gendered character, for example, finds that *To a Lady* begins as does *To Cobham*

> by introducing the premise of the changeableness of human character, which it proceeds to elaborate in its long central section. It turns near its conclusion to the efficacious category of the ruling passion, which serves as the basis for a final generalization. And it ends with a predictable but in some respects extraneous tribute to the exemplary character to whom the epistle is addressed. These structural similarities might lead us to expect to read the poems in the same way, but strangely enough, as we shall find, their effects and assumptions are substantially different. The failure of the parallelism is sex-linked. In applying his paradoxical theory of human character to the 'softer Man' (272), Pope makes women the scapegoats of his ideological dilemma. The misogyny of the poem can be directly linked to this problematic.[9]

Brown inverts Warburton's position by arguing that the inconsistencies between *To Cobham* and *To a Lady* are the consequence of an ideological misrepresentation of women in which similar poetic structures yield dissimilar results. If, that is, Warburton sees the same explanatory principles yielding different "compositions," Brown sees parallel forms of "composition" yielding unequal explanations of gendered character. This inversion permits Brown to identify the blindness of Warburton's reading, since the ideological dilemma Brown speaks of is one that permits Pope to stabilize male character only by imputing "characterlessness" to women. The structural similarities between *To Cobham* and *To a Lady* thus signify a misrepresentation of women, and by extension, of men. Neither men nor women, that is, are correctly represented, insofar as correct representation would imply that Pope conveys a truth about masculinity or femininity free from sexist or classist ideology. But as women suffer most from the effects of Pope's ideologically motivated portrait, they may be said to be misrepresented in a way men are not. The portraits of *To a Lady* are, in other words, ideological manipulations of female character rather than its simple figurative expression.

Brown's analysis forces us to ask what the specifics of subjectivity in *To Cobham* and *To a Lady* are, and whether either sex can ever have a positive identity in Pope's ruminations on gendered character. Ellen Pollak, in her reading of *To a Lady*, gives a powerfully restrictive answer to the last half of this question when she writes:

> For all her variability, woman in Pope's text invariably functions as at once a sign of her own lack and an alibi for the primacy of a masculine presence. She may usurp fictitious identities, may even pretend—like Atossa—to the tyrannical force of masculinity and burn herself out in the very passion by which she resists annihilation; or she may disappear, "ladylike," inside the contours of another subjectivity; but identity is finally conferred on her only within the terms of a hegemonic coupling in which she is both a part and a mirror, or counterpart, of a presence not her own.[10]

This response is like Brown's insofar as it sees character differences between the two epistles as a sex-linked phenomenon. Pollak's claim, though, goes further: her reading identifies the constructedness of female identity in the *Moral Epistles* only in relation to a hegemonic masculinity that successfully disables any representation of woman as a presence or totality in her own right. Such a reading underestimates the possibility that male and female subjects may be similarly generated as nonstable presences, especially if, as I will argue, the same figurative practices regulate Pope's male and female characters. Pollak is right to point out the negativity of Pope's representation of women, but her argument that female identity in the epistles can be "conferred on [woman] only within the terms of a hegemonic coupling in which she is both a part and a mirror, or counterpart, of a presence not her own" fails to account both for the similar formal constraints on Pope's male and female characters and for the possibility that Pope's models of masculinity are themselves riven by the instability of their own claims to coherence. Pollak's arguments about *To a Lady* are a complex modern response to two old questions, questions that Boyce's generic definition of the character evades. Is the male character analyzed in *To Cobham* only male, or may it without prejudice be expanded to describe a more inclusive idea of humanity? Are the criticisms aimed at women in *To a Lady* essential criticisms, or does the figure of woman in this poem represent a more generalized humanity, as some have proposed?[11] Pollak's answers to these questions make the figurative processes producing male subjectivity in the *Epistles* more male specific than they would otherwise be if Pollak's argument did not find its version of sexual difference in an already antecedent epistemological difference.

The difficulty with this debate over the relative value of male and female character is that it remains locked within an understanding of gender in which "male" and "female" are seen not just as *opposite* terms, but as terms whose only possible relation is and remains one of opposition within a closed gender hierarchy. This limitation explains why I have chosen to read these two terms as deriving from similar epistemological pressures at work in the two *Epistles*; it is also why I will attempt to displace the boundaries of this argument by examining in some detail the figural bases that support Pope's polemical characters. As I read them, Pope's two epistles on character are most concerned with ratifying a reliable difference between male and female that his works cannot, finally, sustain.

Male Character and Consistent Inconsistency

If indeed the two epistles use a similar rhetorical strategy to derive male and female character, we should outline that strategy and specify its distinctive features. To do this, though, we must first understand the sex-specific ideological contentions that underlie Pope's constructions of masculinity. The immediate analytical challenge of Pope's first moral epistle, *To Cobham*, can be found in the poem's Argument about *"the* Knowledge *and* Characters *of* Men" (13), which questions just what we can know about male character.[12] The poem quickly generates its own idea of masculinity based on the convergence of masculine actions and passions. *To Cobham's* first few verse paragraphs lay out a method of philosophical inquiry that dissociates apparently stable personality traits from actual male actions. These lines establish a noncontinuous relationship between what may appear to be a cause (personality) and its apparent result (action). They also deny our ability to theorize both abstractly and meaningfully about male character:

> Yes, you despise the man to Books confin'd,
> Who from his study rails at human kind;
> Tho' what he learns, he speaks and may advance,
> Some general maxims, or be right by chance.
>
> (1–4)

According to Pope, Cobham reserves his disgust for the man who reasons abstractly upon humanity in general, since that man's conclusions become only accidentally appropriate to individual cases. Upon closer study, the connection between people and events turns out to be coincidence, but the relationships Pope wishes explicitly to disarticulate are those in which an individual is assigned to a particular social role:

> The coxcomb bird, so talkative and grave,
> That from his cage cries Cuckold, Whore, and
>   Knave,
> Tho' many a passenger he rightly call,
> You hold him no Philosopher at all.
>
> (5–8)

The first eight lines of Pope's poem deal with both traditionally male and female roles, so that Cobham seems to critique a more general concept of humanity. But between the first and second verse paragraphs, Pope silently substitutes "men" for the more inclusive "humanity," and it is only at this point that Pope's poem really concerns itself with "the knowledge and characters of" its sexually differentiated subject. Sexual differentiation thus takes place in an interstice between "human kind" and "man" that Pope never formally opens. Consequently, sexual difference appears in *To Cobham* without ever being explicitly articulated *as* difference.

It is only with this unstated and exclusive distinction in place that bookish philosophers who draw their knowledge of men from texts can err in their statements about men and male identity, but they do so no more than hard-core empiricists who believe in the accuracy of their own observations:

> And yet the fate of all extremes is such,
> Men may be read, as well as Books too much.

To Observations which ourselves we make,
We grow more partial for th' observer's sake;
To written Wisdom, as another's, less:
Maxims are drawn from Notions, these from Guess.

(9–14)

Pope rejects abstract theories of male character as they appear in books and inherited notions. He also seems to reject the observational basis of empirical knowledge because our own "partial" observations are both incomplete and overvalued. But Pope introduces his own empirical model for knowing character on the heels of this first rejection:

There's some Peculiar in each leaf and grain,
Some unmark'd fibre, or some varying vein:
Shall only Man be taken in the gross?
Grant but as many sorts of Mind as Moss.

(15–18)

At first reading, these verses seem to register an obstacle to knowledge in the form of the ungeneralizable particular, but they also imply a capacity to particularize general forms by grasping the "peculiarity" "in each leaf and grain," or at least to know that such peculiarity exists even if in "unmark'd" form. Pope needs this sort of empirical principle for his analysis of male character to work: the implicit contradiction between one mind having both "partial observations" and an understanding that "minds are knowable as moss is knowable," far from disabling *To Cobham*, actually gives us a key to the poem's explanatory strategy. Pope's lines do several things here. To begin with, they describe a system in which the epistemological schemata of characters ("cuckolds," "whores," and "knaves") remain stable while their correspondence to particular bodies or subjects remains at best only one of probability. Second, they question the self-evident truthfulness of immediate observations. Most importantly, these lines ostensibly limit the scope of Pope's inquiry into the psychology of male character (for the most part, but there are a few telling exceptions to this rule in the persons of Narcissa and the female crone at the poem's end) while reserving the right to illuminate his chosen field with knowledge like that of the natural sciences and of natural history.[13] These occasional gestures to something beyond a purely subjective or affective understanding of men help Pope create what will become one of the major thematic maneuvers in *To Cobham*, namely a blending of Pope's intuitive analyses of male character with Pope's own brand of empiricism, which thus allows both empiricism and psychology a potentially reciprocal analytical status. By breaking the links of an easy cause-and-effect correspondence between male personality and observed action, Pope makes it impossible to have a simple empirical understanding of male character as a collection of observed particulars, but by enhancing his character studies with purportedly empirical observations, the poet leaves himself the possibility of grounding an empirically certain knowledge of men and of figurally appropriating a kind of explanatory strategy different from that of personal opinion.

This is the kind of explanation that would confer meaningful correspondence between a character of men and a study of moss. Neither psychological theorizing nor unmediated observations explain why our acts cannot be reasoned out:

> On human actions reason tho' you can,
> It may be reason, but it is not man:
> His Principle of action once explore,
> That instant 'tis his Principle no more.
> Like following life thro' creatures you dissect,
> You lose it in the moment you detect.

(35–40)

The analogy between reason and dissection may not express the underlying cause of a man's behavior, but the simile does explain just how much we can know about this principle and its results. Pope's simile likens the process of reasoning on character to the empirical scientific practice of dissection and thus sets up an equivalence between the kind of knowledge reasoning produces and the kind of knowledge an empirical practice can provide. Pope's simile also implies that reasoning, like dissection, actively interferes with the observed object or practice and, as a consequence, puts an end to the possibility of objectivity. Most importantly, though, this passage argues that something like empiricism does produce knowledge of male character, however limited that knowledge may be, and it is this practice (like but not identical to empirical observation) that works throughout the poem to give Pope's observations on male character the force of objective utterances.

The distinguishing features of Pope's masculine character will be, then, its heterogeneity and unpredictability: "That each from others differs, first confess; / Next that he varies from himself no less" (19–20). We can know that a man will change, but we cannot calculate the permutations of his character because of the problematic identity against which variations would have to be measured. Even the man observing men can, according to Pope's logic, claim no special objective authority for his views because "the diff'rence is as great between / The optics seeing, as the objects seen" (23–24). Indeed, Pope's credentials as an observer would here be doubly suspect, since an ordinary observer has only his (or her?) direct perceptions of men to doubt, but Pope as author not only has to doubt his own perceptions, he also has to worry about the way he represents those perceptions in his poetry. Mentioning his own "optics" may show Pope's sensitivity to the problem and serve as proof of his empirical skepticism, but the effect is still a negative one that implicates Pope as observer in the distorting effects of his own analysis. This distortion would perhaps be an insurmountable problem for Pope if he were to admit explicitly that it applied to himself or to his poem, but the alliance between Pope's psychologizing and empiricizing strategies helps to open a space for Pope's own claims to authority.

Pope disallows in turn both the affective principles and the empirical observations, which, when taken together, provide almost all of the categorical knowledge that a generic character sketch based on observation could provide, as we see in *To Cobham:*

> Judge we by Nature? Habit can efface,
> Int'rest o'ercome, or Policy take place:
> By Actions? Those Uncertainty divides:
> By Passions? these Dissimulation hides:
> Opinions? they still take a wider range:
> Find, if you can, in what you cannot change.
>
> (168–73)

Male character is too changeable for a consistent psychology to emerge. Any given observation of a man's actions or passions gives only (and sometimes duplicitously) the action of that moment, and by the same token, empirical observations give simply the action or passion in itself, without any reliable explanatory gloss on that action's or passion's origin or purpose. Worse, there seems to be no way in which to coordinate a series of empirical observations of men in the process of having character. At its most skeptical, Pope's poem suggests that a sequence of observed actions and possible passions will have only a random, associational value in relation to each other, and the logical extension of this line of argument is that any apparently meaningful pattern arising from such an observed series of male actions and passions would, instead of signifying unity at some interpretive level (for instance, at that of the ruling passion), be only the chance effect of meaningfulness deriving from the contingent alignment of random elements. So many of the poem's first hundred lines are devoted to this uncertainty about man's ability to be known that we may wonder about Pope's motive for presenting his epistle as a study at all. If, after all, it is "In vain the Sage, with retrospective eye, / Would from th' apparent What conclude the Why" (51–52), why does Pope bother with a text that can only misrepresent his subject?

Pope's aim is twofold. The apparent contradiction between dispersing male character into its unknowable particulars just before presenting a moral evaluation of that character allows Pope the interpretive advantage of formulating a necessary myth of comprehensible *and* coherent male subjectivity.[14] This maneuver in its turn permits him to limit the field of play of his subject and helps to give his moral judgments the force of descriptive utterances. In other words, Pope creates a hypothetically coherent subject against the background of his own skepticism, as he does with his inconsistent but "plain rough Hero" whose contradictory actions can only be interpreted by Pope's putative addressee as intentional, while Pope knows that "Alas! in truth the man but chang'd his mind, / Perhaps was sick, in love, or had not din'd" (78–80). The epistemological move of generalizing towards a state in which all possible observations of men would have to exist legitimizes Pope's own evaluations of male character and makes it possible to present this particular kind of knowledge as deriving from male character. Those contradictions involved in trying to study "The Fool" who "lies hid in inconsistencies" (129) inevitably infect every possible study of man, and since Pope acknowledges the problem, he can recoup the explanatory power he may have seemed to lose by beginning such a study in the first place without at the same time having explicitly to acknowledge that his essay orchestrates the same inconsistency giving it its rhetorical persuasiveness.

This inconsistency never really disappears from *To Cobham*, but Pope manages to exploit the contradiction between observable male actions and deeper male motives simply by asserting an ordering principle that reconciles all differences.[15] Indeed, Pope turns "with considerable abruptness"[16] to this principle as a means of unifying his dispersed male character:

> Search then the Ruling Passion: There, alone,
> The Wild are constant, and the Cunning known;
> The Fool consistent, and the False sincere;
> Priests, Princes, Women, no dissemblers here.
>
> (174–77)

The ruling passion provides an epistemological justification for any kind of figural or moral equivalence Pope chooses to assert in either *To Cobham* or *To a Lady* because its very open-endedness permits it to accommodate whatever poetic means may be necessary to produce the knowledge of character Pope needs to underwrite his gender hierarchy. The ruling passion reconciles chance occurrences and psychological uncertainties with the intuitive insight that allows character as a genre to transform a transitory observation into a timeless truth, and it eliminates the possibility that Pope's self-dividing male character will resolve into the disaster of radically irreconcilable "masculinities" by assuring us that whatever a male character may be, it will always be a stable function of its own contradictions.

This doubled system of psychological and empirical interpretation serves Pope by creating a set of mutually correspondent inconsistencies or contradictions that support those interpretive tacks he chooses to take. Empiricism cannot, for instance, reduce to simple human opinion or "partial observation," because if it does we lose that disinterested capacity for reflection which will eventually culminate in the ruling passion and which provides the generic foundation of character itself. The difficulty Pope never quite explains his way around, though, is that "To Observations which ourselves we make, / We grow more partial for th' observer's sake" (11–12).

In other words, this realization does not affect the confidence with which Pope's narrator announces the existence and reliability of the ruling passion. In the world of *To Cobham*, there is always an ideal space set aside, so that somewhere objective references exist outside of the emotive intentions of the male mind, even if that mind is the poet's. In effect, Pope's poem implies that objectivity is possible even as the poem's narrator denies such a possibility.

With a potentially empirical poetic framework in place, male emotions (those wildly rotating passions) become something Pope can write about as if they were lived and accurately representable experience for the characters Pope uses as examples of masculinity. When, for example, the causes of Caesar's momentous decisions seem to resolve into being "beaten" or "drunk," Pope admonishes caution in assigning a reason:

> Ask why from Britain Caesar would retreat?
> Caesar himself might whisper he was beat.
> Why risk the world's great empire for a Punk?
> Caesar perhaps might answer he was drunk.
> But, sage historians! 'tis your task to prove
> One action Conduct; one, heroic Love.
>
> (81–86)

What, though, remains constant here is the reliable uncertainty principle that limits the causes of Caesar's actions to a containable set of alternatives, and whether or not even Caesar knows why he acted as he did is less important than the possibility that the cause *may* be knowable as being "beaten" or "drunk." Pope does not claim absolute certainty, but neither does he claim a disabling uncertainty.

This knowledge of emotion mediated as empirical data constitutes a privileged fund of information about male character that Pope weds to the potential for a validly empirical knowledge of man. If, for Pope, it is "True, some are open, and to all men known; / Others so very close, they're hid from none; (So Darkness strikes the sense no less than Light)" (110–12), then the transformation of masculine character traits such as being open or closed into traits in the first place, into ontological markers with an internal consistence borrowed from a repeatable and externalized sensory experience such as the perception of light, helps tactically to disguise an assertion about male character as factual, systematic knowledge of masculinity.[17] An empirically validated psychology also helps to give Pope's male characters the illusion of being ontologically authentic by virtue of their unpredictable but accurately figured emotions. After all, if Pope's theory of the ruling passion allows male characters at their deepest level to seem ontologically stable rather than socially contingent, then the nonnecessary relationship between sex and character may be hidden behind the mask of a masculinity that presents itself as observable and that already incorporates this contingency as a controllable function internal to itself. Empiricism and psychology interact to produce an autonomous array of masculine positions, and it is these positions which appear to generate an ontologically stable male gender. We may never, that is, be certain that causes are really causes in Pope's masculine fantasy, but we can be certain of the consistent interrelations between those signifying practices associated with masculinity.

Pope and the Synecdochic Woman

The unifying feature of masculine character in *To Cobham* turns out to be consistency at the deep level of the ruling passion, but *To Cobham* suggests that while the pattern of consistency remains constant from man to man, the specific examples of passion are significantly nonidentical with each other. If men are as different as

species of moss, then so are their governing passions. The case for
women in *To a Lady* is famously different:

> In Men, we various Ruling Passions find,
> In Woman, two almost divide the kind;
> Those, only fix'd, they first or last obey,
> The Love of Pleasure, and the Love of Sway.
>
> (207–10)

The categorical finality of these lines echoes throughout the poem
and should, if Pope's gender epistemology is consistent, prove ana-
lytically useful in reading the poem's female characters. In Papillia,
for example, we see an instance of feminine variability:

> wedded to her doating spark, [she]
> Sighs for the shades—"How charming is a Park!"
> A Park is purchas'd, but the Fair he sees
> All bath'd in tears—"Oh odious, odious Trees!"
>
> (37–40)

Papillia's actions seem a simple contradiction of her desires, but we
may read her wish for a park as an exercise both of the love of
pleasure and of the love of sway, since she gets what she wants and
directs her lover as she pleases. Her contradictory behavior allows
her to keep her spark guessing as to her motives, and it also allows
her renewed opportunities to exercise her influence over him. In
other words, the contradiction in Papillia's actions actually exemplifies the two female passions. The difficulty in Papillia's case, of
course, comes in telling one kind of love from the other, but inasmuch as Papillia conforms to the poem's expectation that she will
vary, this difficulty reinforces Papillia's ability to stand in as an

example of expected female character. The ruling passion is, consequently, less important in its own right than it is as a symbol of typically female behavior. By varying reliably between contradictory impulses, Papillia presents a typical example of the kind of action by which she can be known in the poem.

Such typification of possible female activity, and thus of possible identity, lies at the heart of *To a Lady*'s method. My thesis here is that the figure of synecdoche governs Pope's representations of female characterlessness by substituting Pope's own evaluation of a woman's character for observed instances of that character. In *To a Lady*, synecdoche, or the figural relation that mediates between part and whole, both underlies and undermines the apparent chance association of observations within the poem's field of vision that would otherwise constitute a metonymical relationship based on external contiguity or coincidence. In *To a Lady*'s case, the instance that reveals a woman's character is to life as part is to whole; Pope's strategy is to replace the variables of lived experience with a string of static moments. If Pope thus privileges synecdoche over metonymy, seemingly contiguous and unrelated observations of feminine behavior become instead deliberate rewritings of that behavior.

Synecdoche, which a young Jonathan Culler describes as "the most basic rhetorical figure," is the building block of metaphor:

> Metaphor is a combination of two synecdoches: it moves from a whole to one of its parts to another whole which contains that part, or from a member to a general class and then back again to another member of that class.[18]

Metaphor is an assertion of identity; it seeks to elucidate the hidden analogical relationship, the hidden unity underlying apparent dissimilarities. By standing in a synecdochic relationship to each other, the parts of a metaphor imply some greater whole apparent through the rhetorical operation of the figure. Metonymy, on the other hand, is that figural relationship "based on a merely accidental or contingent connexion,"[19] which juxtaposes its elements without premeditation; metonymy is the figure par excellence of randomness and chance. In the rhetorical world of *To a Lady*, terms standing in a metonymic relation to each other do so only as a function of proximity: as accidents of contiguity, the terms of metonymy serve no intentional authorial purpose. As such, metonymy functions as the figure of objective truth for Pope; if instances of female character are aligned metonymically, then those instances are impartial, and whatever objective reality such instances convey may be regretted, but not mitigated. Above all, such instances may not be discounted as the product of a vested or prejudiced authorial perspective. Synecdoche, as opposed to metonymy, would thus be the figure that calls into question the disinterestedness of Pope's observations, and identifying synecdoche as the principal figure of *To a Lady* would also call into question the obviousness of the trope of objective observation. Since objectivity is an integral factor in the generic tradition to which *To a Lady* belongs, the rhetorical constitution of such a genre thus becomes coextensive with Pope's occluded authorial presence.

To a Lady is, of course, part of that long history of poems which conform generally to the generic constraints of the character sketch. If we recall Benjamin Boyce's advice that the character "is to be imagined as alive and individual; but because he is to be seen only in those situations that reveal his dominant moral or psychological habit, the picture will be eclectic, the shadowing heightened," we will recall that what makes a character sketch generically distinct is its faithfulness to reality, its ability to present the essential truth of a character to us. What may pass unremarked in Boyce's definition is the degree to which an authorial intention underwrites the apparent randomness of the observed scene. If, after all, the character is made to appear in scenes showing her "dominant moral or psychological habit," then the author's intervention will effectively determine the context for any impressions the reader receives. It may be helpful to think of the act of representation in *To a Lady* as a scene of Althusserian interpellation: as Pope invokes example after example of female character, the very act of invocation ceases to register explicitly as part of the poem's action and instead becomes an act of simultaneous constitution/subjugation. Female character, or more exactly, the lack thereof, is thus constitutive of the female subject as seen from the perspective of Pope's authorial presence. If, in other words, Pope's character sketches are ideological in nature, the nature of such ideology, at least in *To a Lady*, is to constitute precisely such examples of female character as we find in Pope's poem. Insofar as the "factitiousness" of female character remains unexamined, Pope's project succeeds.[20]

Pope's early observation that "How many Pictures of one Nymph we view, / All how unlike each other, all how true!" (5–6) is itself the most potent typifying tactic *To a Lady* employs, since it is in these lines that Pope quietly establishes the neutral universality of the gaze from which the poet's moral precepts on women will issue. This view of one woman's inconstancy expresses a certain amazement at the nature of female character, but Pope's observation itself never questions its own ability to represent the truth of the nymph's self-difference or to represent inconsistency as a function of femininity. The act of viewing, in other words, evaluates its object without itself ever taking on a value. Whereas in *To Cobham* Pope explicitly problematizes the position of the author/observer,[21] in *To a Lady*, the author's unreliable presence fades from the poem's consciousness to be replaced by a series of apparently stable and self-representative observations. But in *To a Lady*, Pope never gestures towards this disappearance as a problem that entangles the "optics seeing" and the "objects seen."[22] Instead, *To a Lady* replaces the problematic observer, first with a self-confident artist who "paints" feminine extravagance in the person of a charming female, and then with a series of equally self-confident imperatives that direct the reader's attention away from Pope's mediating poetic presence toward the objects of Pope's transparent authorial gaze. Pope as the painter who in one verse paragraph announces that "Whether the Charmer sinner it, or saint it, / If Folly grows romantic, I must paint it" (15–16) becomes in the next verse paragraph an imperative voice that sets the terms for perceiving and valuing female character:

> Come then, the colours and the ground prepare!
> Dip in the Rainbow, trick her off in Air,
> Chuse a firm Cloud, before it fall, and in it
> Catch, ere she change, the Cynthia of this minute.
>
> (17–19)

The "Cynthia of this minute" seems to pose a tremendous challenge to the observing artist who would "trick her off in Air" using the delightful but ephemeral colors of the rainbow, but the narrative injunctions to "Come," "prepare," "Dip," "trick off," "Chuse," and "Catch" imply that women are available subjects for some material process of representation and that some generic truth about women is materially available to the observant man. Pope thus associates women in *To a Lady* with an observable materiality that allows the narrative gaze unproblematic access to those women, but what the authorial imperative hides here is its own standpoint, its own perspective as masculine and therefore authoritative.[23] The "Cynthia of this minute" will always be a function of this perspective, even as the explicit authorial agent establishing that perspective withdraws from the poem's foreground and leaves only the trail of its gaze to define its female object. The acting agent for much of Pope's poem thus becomes this authorial command. Pope's reader is directed to "See Sin in State, majestically drunk" (69); to "Turn then from Wits; and look on Simo's Mate" (101); to "Yet mark the fate of a whole Sex of Queens!"; to "See how the World its Veterans rewards!" (243). The authorial imperative invokes an author who is also a reliable observer for its power, but by replacing the problematic figure of the poet/observer with an imperious and unanswerable command to act, Pope transforms the action of judging women's characters into the action of observing women. As a consequence, these authorial imperatives so structure Pope's poem that the injunction to observe and the observation itself collapse into each other. The consequence for the reader is that the reader's consciousness necessarily becomes imbricated as part of, if not entirely extensive with, the perspective of the vanished artist. It is, after all, through the medium of these imperatives that the reader is incorporated as a function of the poem. By observing the imperative, the reader establishes his or her agency within the poem's fictional space; what we might thus call the readerly subject is defined as a displacement of the authorial imperative onto the position of the reader.

These imperatives thus help to create the illusion of observation that allows Pope to specify the details making up a generic character of women. Beginning at line 101, for instance, *To a Lady* gives us a quick succession of female types who exemplify the failures and inconsistencies of female identity:

> Turn then from Wits; and look on Simo's Mate,
> No Ass so meek, no Ass so obstinate:
> Or her, that owns her Faults, but never mends,
> Because she's honest, and the best of Friends:
> Or her, whose life the Church and Scandal share,
> For ever in a Passion, or a Pray'r:
> Or her, who laughs at Hell, but (like her Grace)
> Cries, "Ah! how charming if there's no such place!"
> Or who in sweet vicissitude appears
> Of Mirth and Opium, Ratafie and Tears,

The daily Anodyne, and nightly Draught,
To kill those foes to Fair ones, Time and Thought.
                                                    (101–12)

Difference, with its potential for distinct identity, fails to register as
difference in this passage because each example Pope cites turns
out to be the same example of female conduct. The apparent arbitrariness of Pope's repeated "Or her . . . Or her . . . Or her," an
arbitrariness that gives the impression of random observation and
selection from within the totality of the poet's field of sight, never
fails to produce a woman who is somehow the same as all the other
women in Pope's sampling. More importantly, what appear to be
individual, reliably recorded examples of women's contradictions
and moral failings turn out, on closer examination, to be categorical reductions of female characterlessness masquerading as observed
moments in the relation between critic and object. The concrete
instance of a particular woman's inconstancy—for instance, the
immoral (or amoral)[24] woman who cries "Ah! how charming" when
liberated from the potential retribution of hell—is really a typification of *all* possible ways in which this woman can act. She moves
predictably between "The daily Anodyne, and nightly Draught"
not just because these "kill those foes to Fair ones, Time and
Thought," but also because Pope's poem allows her no greater range
for action in its observed field. This is what the poem "sees" her
doing when it bids us "look on Simo's Mate" and her crew. For the
poem, this woman's entire identity is thus the example cited, and
the example is specifically and *only* the action cited.

In each of these cases, from Simo's meek and obstinate mate to
the woman who appears in constant (and consistent) oscillation
between "Mirth and Opium, Ratafie and Tears," what Pope gives
us is not, as it may first seem, a metonymically conditioned instance
of the woman's observed characterlessness in which actions are linked
by chance to other individual actions. It is instead a synecdochic

condensation of the times, places, and ways in which these women may act at all, so that what seems to be a listing of contiguous instances proving Pope's proposition becomes, in the poem's epistemological structure, an essentializing metaphor for the entirety of feminine experience and action.[25] Chronological time and charactered identity are, for these women, reduced to a simple, repeated cycle where "The daily Anodyne, and nightly Draught" work consistently. Pope's typical maneuver for each sketch is to substitute a generic evaluation of womanly character for the specific, presumably observable instance that would prove the generic rule.

As we have seen, Pope repeatedly requires gestures of "turning" and "seeing" from his audience, and it is these gestures that allow Pope to consolidate male character and female characterlessness.[26] These deictic gestures give the impression that what is being turned to or seen really exists as an observable moment in the poem's progress. The poem presents these moments as contiguously related instances brought together by the poet's observing eye. But such moments, acting in accord with the generic constraints of a character poem, also produce the substantive and morally determining image of women in general. Understood this way, these quasi-empirical examples of female characterlessness cease to be governed by the disinterested principle of metonymy and instead become part of the figural subterfuge by which morally charged and essentializing attitudes about women and their conduct become objective instances of women caught in the act of characterlessness. The common figural rule motivating these scenes is one in which an apparently random series turns out not to be random at all, so that the shared figural ground for each portrait of a characterless woman becomes that very characterlessness. Apparently verifiable differences from woman to woman all produce this same sort of synecdochic commensurability and show us a trait that is both consistent from one episode of a woman's life to the next *and* also consistently like the characteristic traits of other female personalities.

Pope's account of Queen Caroline practices this kind of reduction even as it chides sycophantic artists for the inauthentic "zeal" of their misrepresentations:

> One certain Portrait may (I grant) be seen,
> Which Heav'n has varnish'd out, and made a *Queen:*
> The same for ever! and describ'd by all
> With Truth and Goodness, as with Crown and Ball:
> Poets heap Virtues, Painters Gems at will,
> And show their zeal, and hide their want of skill.
>
> (181–86)

Pope satirizes such "zeal" as a form of repetition where "Truth and Goodness" and "Crown and Ball" appear again and again in every description. Virtuous qualities and monarchical symbols thus appear side by side without necessarily relating to each other in any essential fashion, so that Caroline's queenly attributes and her putative virtues become external features of the portrait rather than interior qualities specific to the woman. This figural association, one easily established by "heaping" virtues and gems indiscriminately on the same object, produces an image of monarchical authority based on metonymic coincidence rather than on metaphoric essence. But this metonymic strategy is precisely the one Pope uses in his own sketch of Caroline. For *To a Lady*, Caroline becomes little more than a repetition of the same bad portrait "Which Heav'n has varnish'd out, and made a *Queen,*" and it is this repetitive association of images that stands in for the woman herself, so that the randomness of metonymy becomes through repetition a synecdochic expression of the Queen's identity. By establishing the queen's portrait as "certain," Pope's poem thus replaces Caroline with an image and fixes that image in the kind of representative moment that signifies the queen's femaleness and her similarity to the other women in *To a Lady*. Caroline does, in the poem's terms, indeed become "the same for ever," because to be "certain" or "the same" is to be a woman.

In effect, Pope's sketches suggest that a woman's life reduces faithfully to the examined moment. Such temporal compression agrees with the general constraints of a character, whether male or female, and works simultaneously to transform a series of contiguous instances into the coherence of a female character while making female identity the end result of this series of restricting substitutions. If, for example, we look at "great Atossa," we see a woman "Scarce once herself, by *turns* all Womankind!" (116, my emphasis). In her case, though, it is an entire life that has been compressed into one representative moment. This sort of permanent metaphorical present tense allows Pope to define Atossa as one "Who, with herself, or others, from her birth / Finds all her life one warfare upon earth" in which she "Shines, in exposing Knaves, and painting Fools, / Yet is, whate'er she hates and ridicules" (117–20). Atossa's life is a series of these "ridiculous" moments. She will, for instance, respond in exactly the same manner regardless of the array of differences present in any particular moment in her history. Atossa's identity as an inconsistent woman is the *same* identity from moment to moment, regardless of circumstance: there is no order of action or being too anomalous to be consumed and processed by her overwhelmingly consistent inconstancy:

> Her ev'ry turn with Violence pursu'd,
> Nor more a storm her Hate than Gratitude.
> To that each Passion turns, or soon or late;
> Love, if it makes her yield, must make her hate:
> Superiors? death! and Equals? what a curse!
> But an Inferior not dependant? worse.
> Offend her, and she knows not to forgive;
> Oblige her, and she'll hate you while you live:
> But die, and she'll adore you—Then the Bust

And Temple rise—then fall again to dust.
Last night, her Lord was all that's good and great,
A Knave this morning, and his will a Cheat.

(131–42)

It literally makes no difference whether the figure to which Atossa responds is male or female, the generic "you" or "her Lord," and while these lines seem to register a degree of class difference between superiors or equals and "Inferiors not dependant," the following couplet on "offending and obliging" assimilates any difference Atossa may perceive between classes in the way she acts towards classed individuals. If "you" offend her, "she knows not to forgive," but "Oblige her, and she'll hate you while you live." Atossa thus orbits between two emotions that are both finally a form of hate, and while she appears to differ by loving and hating her lord, both emotions are based on the same blindness and misapprehension informing her response to any situation and lead inevitably to the same result. For "Full sixty years the World has been her Trade," but the only result of a lifetime's experience is that she becomes "The wisest Fool much Time has ever made" (123–24). And since each instance describing her life relates some example of the same "foolishness," time itself makes no mark on Atossa's career. In short, Atossa's life is a chronology, but one consistent with the generalizing constraints a character portrait imposes upon its subject: if a generically recognizable character is to result, the examples that convey one's essential traits to the reader must present the same traits regardless of the moment. Pope's narrative of Atossa's life must thus move from one moment to the next, but the moral category of "Atossa" has to remain the same at all times in that life. This stasis results from the substitution of one putatively representative instance for the entirety of her life. Such synecdochic substitution is characteristic of the formal limits to female identity in *To a Lady* and of the genre to which *To a Lady* belongs. Pope is thus disingenuous in his assertion that "How many Pictures of one Nymph we view, / All how unlike each other, all how true!" Just as different pictures of the nymph converge into one truth, so difference as a meaningful category becomes the reiteration of an identifying, and finally, reifying, moment. Pope appears to describe the plenitude of a woman's life, but in reality he compresses that life into one representative instance; instance thus becomes to life as part is to whole, and the synecdochic woman emerges through and as repetition.

Even the ideal woman of Pope's imagination conforms to synecdochic regulation. When Pope invokes his helpmate, we find her "blest with Temper, whose unclouded ray / Can make to morrow chearful as to day" (257–58) and thus able to render one day identical to the next:

> She, who can love a Sister's charms, or hear
> Sighs for a Daughter with unwounded ear;
> She who ne'er answers till a Husband cools,
> Or, if she rules him, never shows she rules;
> Charms by accepting, by submitting sways,
> Yet has her humour most, when she obeys;
> Lets Fops or Fortune fly which way they will;
> Disdains all loss of Tickets, or Codille;
> Spleen, Vapours, or Small-pox, above them all,
> And Mistress of herself, tho' China fall.
>
> (259–68)

The ideal wife holds a unique position in To a Lady's catalogue. Given the poem's laudatory tone, one would assume that she represents an appropriate model for female conduct, standing as she does in general contradistinction to the rest of the women sketched. She is even-tempered, modest, submissive, intelligent, and self-disciplined. She cooly transcends the vicissitudes of misfortune and disease, and she remains equally complacent in the face of a distempered husband or broken plate. Seen in this light, it is easy to agree with Howard Weinbrot that

> The portrait of the lady in her family life shows that she has learned the lesson Pope has taught—that being a queen in public life destroys women, whose proper sphere is private life. In so learning, the lady also becomes the female model of the *discordia concors*, of what Pope again, in his own note, calls "The Picture of an estimable Woman, with the best kinds of contrarieties."[27]

But this wifely figure is certainly more than the timely beneficiary of Pope's insights. Besides questioning the two-dimensional character of Weinbrot's domestic space, we should note that "the female model of the *discordia concors*," the woman who becomes a figure for the reconciliation of contrarieties, employs her contradictions to a purpose, unlike the poem's other women. Papillia, Simo's mate, and Atossa differ from themselves profitlessly; their contradictory behavior finally destroys any chance of either a stable personality or any degree of meaningful personal autonomy.[28] The ideal wife, on the other hand, marshals her contrarieties smoothly to become the final authority in her household. Her "proper sphere" may be private life (since public life is by definition antithetical to women), as Weinbrot suggests, but what Weinbrot fails to emphasize is her radical potential as compared to the poem's other subjects. "She, who ne'er answers till a Husband cools, / Or, if she rules him, never shows she rules" has the advantage of choice. Unlike her husband, who acts only in response to his wife's initiative, or the other women, who lack the character to recognize their own best interests, the wife utilizes her contradictory capacities in an almost Machiavellian fashion to gain her will regardless of the circumstance. For good or ill, she who can remain "Mistress of herself, tho' China fall" is the most efficient agent in Pope's poem.

Her ability to reconcile the contrarieties of her character makes the ideal wife something of an anomaly. Her status as a moral example cuts her off from that class of which she might otherwise act as representative. She, unlike others, "Lets Fops or Fortune fly which way they will; / Disdains all loss of Tickets, or Codille," but her very moral exemplarity prevents her from enjoying a thematic resemblance to the poem's other women.[29] In one of the poem's most important paradoxes, the ideal wife's character prevents her from acting as a representative member of womankind. Because she is such a rarity, she cannot stand in a synecdochic relation to the rest of the poem's women. From a thematic perspective, it is as if the woman who reconciles her own contradictions can no longer be recognized as a woman. True to Pope's argument, as well as to his prejudice, she remains sui generis, a fantasy of the poem's own unfolding.

In effect, this passage rejects the principle of synecdoche at one level only to reaffirm it at another: if, to be a model of domestic virtue this woman must be morally different from all others, then that difference is one the poem cannot sustain at the rhetorical level. The balanced neoclassical antithesis of the couplet, "Charms by accepting, by submitting sways / Yet has her humour most, when she obeys" might indeed suggest that this woman has taken Pope's morality to heart if she were not such a neatly symmetrical antithesis herself of the characterless woman. Pope uses *epanados*, or the progressive repetition of a key word—in this case, "by"—to distinguish between two types of feminine conduct.[30] By "accepting" and "submitting" the woman "Charms" and "sways," but as the repetition of "by" makes clear, ruling a husband and being ruled by him collapse into one another and bring us full circle to the ruling female passions of "the love of pleasure and the love of sway."

However benevolent her actions may seem, their consequence is still to have "her humour most." That these actions are ruled by a figure of repetition is also necessary: "never answering until a Husband cools" or "never showing that she rules" are less the wise acts of an ideal wife than a reiteration of the figural parameters of female identity. The virtuous woman is, like Atossa or the queen, a repetition of the same moral instance, but her thematic status demands that the poem set her apart, as if she were not an example of the rule she proves.

Gender and Figure

If we now return to *To Cobham*, we can better understand the synecdochic constraints Pope places on both male and female character.

Philip, duke of Wharton, "Whose ruling Passion was the Lust of Praise" (181) gives us a male passion predicated on lack and misdirected desire, characteristics Pope usually assigns to the women of *To a Lady*. Wharton exhibits the familiar and empirically coded trait of consistent inconsistency structured by affective intent. He is "Born with whate'er could win [praise] from the Wise," but "Women and Fools must like him or he dies" (182–83); his flaw is that "Thus with each gift of nature and of art, / And wanting nothing but an honest heart" (192–93) he grows "all to all, from no one vice exempt, / And most contemptible, to shun contempt; / His Passion still, to covet gen'ral praise, / His Life, to forfeit it a thousand ways" (194–97). Wharton is definitively masculine by Popean standards, as his instability shows. He is exactly like "That very Caesar," who if "born in Scipio's days / Had aim'd like him, by Chastity at praise" (216–17), in direct contradiction to Caesar's actual (and typical) activities. The point, though, is that any moment in Wharton's life is just like any other: Pope takes us from the moment when Wharton is "Born with whate'er could win [praise]" to the instant when "He dies, sad out-cast of each church and state" (204) without encountering a difference in time, place, or station that the poem finds unassimilable. Each moment is synecdochically linked to the next in a way that does not so much suggest similarity as identity, since each moment is an identical example of Wharton's lust for praise. Wharton may appear to embody the diversity of a "real" subject by being "from no one vice exempt" or by using his life to "forfeit [praise] a thousand ways," but the illusion of metonymy, the unintended association of events within the field of the observer's neutral gaze, is itself determined by the same sort of synecdochic compression we encounter in the portrait of Atossa. Pope here inverts the relation between lived experience and generic abstraction by figuring both Wharton and Atossa as if their lives were already structured by the synecdochic principles that ideally derive from "life" to give us the abstraction of "character."[31] Indeed, the hallmark of reality in Pope's epistles is the noncontingency or rejection of randomness that defines the ruling passion and that tailors reality to fit generic identities.

Cobham's life also reduces to a repetition of the same instance, though in his case, the definitive moment is one Pope finds wholly admirable:

> And you! brave COBHAM, to the latest breath
> Shall feel your ruling passion strong in death:
> Such in those moments as in all the past,
> "Oh, save my Country, Heav'n!" shall be your last.
>
> (262–65)

Cobham's patriotic and most typical moment is much like the frugal crone's or Narcissa's, in that the moment of death stands in for all of an individual's most characteristic experiences. The crone

Still tries to save the hallow'd taper's end,
Collects her breath, as ebbing life retires,
For one puff more, and in that puff expires.

(239–41)

while Narcissa's deathbed cry sums up her character as effectively
as Cobham's does his own:

"Odious! in woollen! 'twould a Saint provoke,
(Were the last words that poor Narcissa spoke)
"No, let a charming Chintz, and Brussels lace
"Wrap my cold limbs, and shade my lifeless face:
"One would not, sure, be frightful when one's dead—
"And—Betty—give this Cheek a little Red."

(242–47)

Cobham, Narcissa, and the crone each give us the same sort of
deathbed utterance (that the crone's is wordless does not matter
much to Pope's scheme), in that the action observed adequately
represents the individual life as a whole and is thus appropriate to
a character. Miriam Leranbaum has suggested that Pope praises
Cobham "for dying words which will surely do him credit, in distinct and unique contrast to other characters whose dying words
reveal them as consistently and ignobly self-centred" ("*Opus Magnum*," 65), but there is nothing inherent in the figural constitution
or operation of either male or female characters here to tell us whose
utterance is ultimately superior to the others; what we know from
the method of the *Epistles* is that similar sorts of utterance predi-
cate similar characters and that each utterance can legitimately stand
in for the rest of an individual's life.[32] Differing moral evaluations
of those sketched cannot, I contend, arise from within the category
of character based only on gender, because gender is not a primary

constituent in the rhetorical mechanics of Popean character. This is not to say that moral evaluations between Cobham and Narcissa or the crone cannot be made, only that gender alone is insufficient to support such determinations and that it is class status rather than essential masculinity that allows Cobham his chance to be "admirable."

Clearly, then, male and female character in *To Cobham* and *To a Lady* are less consistently different than Pope's poetry argues them to be. Pollak is right that Pope's idea of "woman" in *To a Lady* is a artificial and nonnecessary one, but, while Pollak does recognize the figural manipulations that ground female identity, she misses the principle of synecdochic equivalence underlying both male and female character. Instead, what the two epistles display is twofold: (1) an anxiety about sexual identity in which male and female come to look much more like each other than Pope's opposition of male character and female characterlessness would suggest, and (2) an inability to keep male and female characters in the epistles from being similarly constituted as "characters" in the Popean language of the character sketch. This inability harks back to Boyce's definition of the character, where an "imaginary person" may step in for a group if he can "be seen only in those situations that reveal his dominant moral or psychological habit" (152). Since neither women nor men can be constituted according to a single, stable set of characteristics, an attempt like Pope's to stabilize one characteristic, in this case the characteristic of "character," necessarily succumbs to the kind of figural slippage we have seen in the two epistles. Gender as a discursive practice in Pope's poems does not, in other words, lend itself to the kind of generic stability Pope's formulation of character requires. The epistles thus enact through their own metaphorical operations a powerful critique of male character and authority.

Pope's challenge in the two epistles is, finally, to produce a readable sexual difference between male and female that is not subject to the dislocations and referential inadequacies inherent to the reading process itself. To succeed, such a project would paradoxically have to convey the rhetorical figures of sexual difference as full presences in their own right, presences that simultaneously distinguish one sex from the other and purvey the truth of that sex without mediating or refracting nature's plenitude through the artifice of language. There is, as we have seen, a direct contradiction between Pope's claim that the ruling passion represents male and female activity sufficiently and his poems' ability to enact masculinity and femininity figurally. The claims that rest on a notion of the ruling passion's adequacy—that men have many passions and women few, that man's life is essentially public and woman's essentially private, that most men have character and most women do not—are constantly belied by the figural similarities giving rise to what Pope calls "male" and "female" identity. Reading the subjects of *To Cobham* and *To a Lady* as subjects developed from the generically distinctive, synecdochically compressed practices of the character sketch, rather than as men and women who somehow achieve gender before the event of the poem itself, means that figural difference or similarity must precede gender difference or similarity. The men and women of Pope's epistles are men and women not so much because that is what they *are*, but because that is what Pope calls them in an effort to install a sexual difference that may not inhere characteristically if the poems are left to their own poetic devices. It is here that the differences in structure and approach Brown speaks of come into play, not so much as signs of an absolute epistemological incompatibility between men and women, but as tokens of Pope's inability to keep male and female gender identities consistently apart and of the anxiety this inability inspires. The logical tenuity of his argument means that the contradictions of his position are, at times, more than his poetry can support. These contradictions are both masked and exposed by the poems' formal characteristics, and it is this double process which impedes a perfect alignment of poetic structure and misogynist intent.

FOUR

Haywood's *Philidore and Placentia,* or What the Eunuch Lost

Insofar as her place in eighteenth-century English literature has been secured, Eliza Haywood's reputation depends upon her work as an amatory novelist, a *romancière* who successfully translates the tradition and conventions of the seventeenth-century French romance novel into English. She is, along with Aphra Behn and Delarivière Manley, most often credited with exploiting and developing the form of the scandalous amatory novel, which gained great popularity toward the close of the 1720s. In his analysis of the genre's history, John J. Richetti notes that

> During the first two decades of the century, the production of original English amatory fiction was relatively small. There was Mrs. Manley, of course, and her very successful naturalization of the French *chronique scandaleuse* to the political controversies of the day. The novels of the long-dead Mrs. Behn continued to be widely read, but the great majority of amatory fiction consisted of translations, mostly of the French. The works of native practitioners did not

really rival translations in popularity until the third decade of the century when the "novels" of Mrs. Eliza Haywood began to appear.[1]

Rounding out the "fair triumvirate of Wit,"[2] as the English poet James Sterling put it in his panegyric on her works, Haywood focused her energies on the sort of exotic and amorous fiction that earned her both a popular audience and also the disdain of such literary monuments as Alexander Pope.[3] Haywood was at her most productive during the 1720s,[4] and it was during this period that she produced one of her more complexly plotted works, *Philidore and Placentia* (1727).

Although available to audiences since 1963, *Philidore and Placentia* has received scant critical attention. Richetti mentions it in passing as "of historical interest only."[5] Michael McKeon examines it briefly in his reading of the role of capital in the emergence of *romance* as an early-eighteenth-century form.[6] The novel is absent from Ros Ballaster's otherwise comprehensive reading of Haywood's works,[7] and Paula Backsheider cites it only briefly in her work on the concept of "esteem."[8] Only Mary Ann Schofield has paid extended attention to *Philidore and Placentia*, and her reading serves principally to place the novel's heroine in the tradition of the "virtuous woman" common to the British romances of this period. To produce this "virtuous woman," Schofield performs a detailed survey of Haywood's romances and concludes that the Haywoodian heroine is a function of her sexual difference from her sometimes less than heroic male counterpart. In her study of Haywood's heroines, Schofield argues that

> In the majority of Haywood's novels, the male is the hunter, the predator and destroyer of female virtue. In a few cases . . . men are honest and true; they manage to remain virtuous and do marry their ladies at the end in true romance fashion.

Primarily, though, the male is only superficially drawn; Haywood's interest is the heroine and her problems, and the male is only considered insofar as he contributes to the woman's dilemmas of self-division.[9]

Philidore, Placentia's lover, is one of those few "honest and true" heroes Schofield describes, but according to Schofield, his very honesty and fidelity reinforce the pattern of male/female relationships that distinguishes Haywood's writing. Because Philidore refuses the role of aggressive male, "Placentia mentally becomes the male in the ensuing courtship"[10] and thus conserves within herself discreet categories of "male" and "female":

[Placentia] philosophically assumes the male role in the love affair between herself and Philidore. The tension inherent in woman, those polarities of submission and aggression, passivity and independence, here in *Philidore and Placentia* are given substance in Placentia's total adoption of the male-like, dominant qualities.[11]

The peculiarity of the above quote derives, I believe, from Schofield's attempt to pose as simultaneously shared and distinct character traits she wishes to see as sex-specific. If, in other words, Placentia must become like a man to maintain her position in a male/female relationship, if she must "adopt male-like qualities" to save the relationship because her man is too polite to act like a man, then whatever it is that makes a man most a man (aggression, independence) is also what it takes for a woman to keep her place in the novel's primary heterosexual relationship. Schofield interprets *Philidore and Placentia* as "a woman-oriented novel" in which "the female characters are far superior to the weaker, controllable males."[12] But Schofield's interpretation depends in its turn on concepts of masculinity and femininity that precede and stabilize those very characteristics which, in themselves, are supposed to distinguish male from female.

I make this argument in part because Schofield's notion of the heroine seems, to me, unnecessarily essentializing, and partly because I wish to thematize and to expose precisely such categories of heterosexually gendered identity. *Philidore and Placentia* strikes me as a unique text in the romance tradition because it plays so fast and loose with the idea of sexual difference, particularly where the male body is concerned.

Structured as a novel in two parts, *Philidore and Placentia, or L'Amour trop Delicat* tells the story of Philidore, the handsome young scion of a noble but degenerate line, and his almost impossibly pure love for the beautiful Placentia, sole mistress of a vast estate and fortune. Framed by this main narrative, in which Philidore denounces himself as unworthy of Placentia and sets sail for the East to lose his passion in the burning Persian climate, is a subplot devoted to a character called the Christian Eunuch, who eventually emerges as Placentia's brother, the Baron Bellamont. In another novelist's hands, the Christian Eunuch might simply serve as a convenient device for exploiting the exotica of a typical Orientalist tale: cruel bashaws, teaming seraglios, beautiful and forbidden mistresses, miserable slaves, and devious eunuchs. Haywood makes full use of each of these devices to stimulate her reader's curiosity and to move her sometimes cumbersome plot from one point to the next, but the Christian Eunuch and his function in a novel dominated by the generic requirements of the romance remain at odds with the typical gender relations underlying the scandalous romance in general. As I will argue in the following chapter, the figure of the Eunuch disturbs the heterosexual context of Haywood's romance. His castration reveals the contingent nature of gender identifications, normally hidden by the seamless heterosexual character of Haywood's amatory fiction; these identifications suddenly become visible, put at risk by the very way Haywood does and does not recuperate the Eunuch as a gendered individual. Further, I will contend that Haywood employs the Eunuch's castrated body as a way to contain the disruptive presence of the male body.

Before we examine the disruptive effect the Eunuch has on the novel's gender system, though, we should consider the parameters within which "male" and "female" become meaningful terms in Haywood's *romance* lexicon. If it is possible to plunge in medias res regarding a character sketch, that is where Haywood begins, with an account of Philidore's unhappy passion for Placentia:

> It was his fate to meet a lady, in a visit he made at the house of a distant relation, with whom he fell so desperately in love that from the first moment of his seeing her, one may date the last of his repose or capacity of acting in a manner any way becoming either his circumstances or education. All those thrilling pleasures, those sweet softnesses with which the dawn of love is generally accompanied were strangers to his heart, and in their room, despair, with all its black attendants, racked him with unceasing anguish.[13]

Because he has no fortune to offer Placentia, Philidore cannot confess his love—but to live apart from his beloved is equally impossible. Like his precursors in the *romance* genre, Philidore's passions are immediate, unswerving, and gratifyingly idealistic.[14] Unlike his precursors, though, Philidore will become his own obstacle to the realization of his love. Since he is unworthy of Placentia while in his proper person, Philidore must literally deface himself so that his natural beauty and breeding do not betray him:

> Never did nature adorn a head with more lovely hair than was his, all which he cut off and in the room of it wore a little periwig of a dark color. His fine and delicate complexion he

disguised with the peel of walnuts insomuch that he appeared of the Egyptian breed. His gay apparel was converted into homely russet, all the fine gentleman into a country boor; and thus transformed, he went to the house of his adored Placentia. (159)

For her part, Placentia fails to notice Philidore, now renamed Jacobin, until she chances to hear him sing one day:

She had not passed many paces from the house before her ears were saluted with the accents of the most harmonious voice she had ever heard. The more she advanced, the more distinct were the notes; and she, who had a great genius to music herself, presently perceived that the person that sung had received his instructions from the best masters. (160)

Once Placentia notices Jacobin, she is also involuntarily drawn to him, just as he is to her:

She, who thought to have asked him some further questions concerning his birth and education, was once or twice about to call him back; but something, which at that time she could not account for, stopped the utterance of her words. . . . The sweetness of the voice and the skill by which it was directed . . . opened her eyes to discern something in Jacobin which till then she had never regarded. . . . In fine, she was charmed with him without knowing she was so, and, insensible of the danger, suffered herself to become a prey to it without the least endeavors for defense. (161–62)

What is remarkable about these passages is that lower class status apparently neutralizes Philidore's masculinity. Until she hears his fine voice and begins to suspect him of being a gentleman, Placentia's sexuality never engages Philidore's in that oppositional, complementary fashion we have come to identify as heterosexual. Philidore is simply another servant doing his duty to her. But class, at least at the thematic level, cannot decisively determine one's sexual response; the moment Placentia perceives that Philidore is "the finest and most just proportioned man in the world" (162) is also the moment that his body evokes an amatory response from hers. Caught unawares, robbed of her speech and will by "something, which at that time she could not account for," Placentia is "charmed" by Philidore in a way that suggests some teleological orientation of female to male. The involuntary nature of this response, indeed, the hackneyed trope of "love at first sight," places heterosexual difference, and not class difference, at the heart of the romance's ideology. Class thus functions here less as a mask hiding heterosexuality than as a conduit insuring that appropriately classed individuals partner each other, and, indeed, most of the plot of *Philidore and Placentia* concerns Haywood's attempts to stabilize her hero's and heroine's class status. The class markers Haywood associates with Philidore belong to those older generic conventions of the romance, while the kind of sexual identity Philidore and Placentia model reflects an emerging concern with the stability of sexual difference, a concern recapitulated in modern terms by Schofield's criticism. The older romance tradition rendered identity in terms of class and social standing—knights, heroes, princes, princesses, and so on. As the late-eighteenth-century author Clara Reeve put it, "the Romance is an heroic fable, which treats of fabulous persons and things"; the "fabulous persons" to whom Reeve refers, especially in the seventeenth-century French tradition from which Haywood's novel is descended, would have been categorized foremost by class.[15] Sexuality for such characters would have been an expression of class standing, not an independent quality. Indeed, as Richetti points out, the drawback of working with elevated characters is that such class status may be too inaccessible for the early-eighteenth-century reader to understand it, or to identify with it:

> The formal changes which prose narrative undergoes [in this period] look impeccably reasonable from this distance, but on the popular level with which we are concerned those formal changes are also a response to a new kind of audience, one unprepared to cope with the sheer bulk and complication of the heroic romance but too 'sophisticated' to be satisfied with chap-books and not so pious as to be content with Bunyan and other popular religious narratives.[16]

The changes in audience expectation that Richetti identifies are those which rewrite the *romance héroïque* as an increasingly recognizable form of the realistic novel. Haywood's contribution to this process is to relocate sexuality within the body as an independent characteristic that will now function, if not beyond the effects of class status, then at least as a means of authenticating identity without exclusive resort to such status.

These scenes also set the pattern for that series of delayed gratifications which characterize early-eighteenth-century amatory fiction. As Ros Ballaster notes,

> romantic fiction constantly renarrates the story of courtship, closing with marriage or betrayal, as though no other period in a woman's life held significance. The pornographic pleasures of romantic fiction are built on a process of persistent textual withholding in which the act of seduction is repeatedly deferred.[17]

I would argue that the serial nature of the seduction scene idealizes what we might call the heterosexual imperative: the mutual and exclusive evocation of male and female bodies by each other. Philidore and Placentia are made for each other because the changing conventions of romance demand (in terms of romantic love) an ineffable link between man and woman. Placentia's inability to articulate her own desire, or, for that matter, to treat desire as a function of individual will and decision, suggests that her relationship to Philidore is either pre- or extradiscursive and that her identity as the novel's heroine is guaranteed by the seduction Philidore inevitably practices upon her. Rank and nobility mark the passing of the romance; heterosexual difference heralds the arrival of the novel.

That this is principally a heterosexual relationship mediated by class is, I think, shown by the notion of Philidore's "just proportions." If a man's body is appropriately proportioned, in relation to what standard or to what activity does "proportion" become a meaningful term? The very notion of proportion depends upon antecedent concepts of purpose and complementarity that define the "heterosexuality" of the romance genre.[18] In an epic, for example, Philidore's body might be justly and primarily proportioned for strength, battle, and conquest, and only secondarily for love and sex, but in the tradition to which Haywood belongs, the male body's single most important purpose is to evoke its natural opposite, the female body. Indeed, nature expresses itself as the correlation of one kind of body to the other. Once Placentia really considers Jacobin/Philidore closely, for example, she is willing to attribute the grace his upbringing and education afford him to his superior physical "loveliness" (162). Philidore's privileged class status as a romance hero is, in this instance, displaced onto his body to mark his masculinity. For Haywood's novel, the physical attraction of sexuality and the moral commitment of love collapse into each other because the difference between man and woman must be purposive rather than arbitrary or contingent. We are so thoroughly conditioned to think in terms of a heterosexual logic that to entertain the idea that sexual differences could be neutral rather than laden with specific purpose is, for many, a ludicrous exercise. But for Haywood's seduction scenes to work as Ballaster describes, male and female must have a compelling, nonarticulated—and therefore natural—relationship to each other. What in other circumstances might seem a social phenomenon must, for Haywood, appear as a natural function of the heterosexual body. Whatever else love is in Haywood's novel, it is as involuntary and bodily a characteristic as sexual desire where the hero and heroine are concerned. Philidore and Placentia are the novel's lovers; any other relationship they enter into must not displace that central convention.

The centrality of the heterosexual love convention makes Haywood's introduction of the Christian Eunuch a remarkable innovation. Near the end of part 1, Philidore, having survived shipwreck, pirates, and a savage tiger (which he dispatches with a single thrust), encounters a beautiful young man fighting for his life against unequal odds. Philidore vanquishes the youth's attackers only to have the youth fall in a dead swoon from loss of blood. Philidore's reaction to this situation is, to say the least, noteworthy:

> The grief of Philidore to see [the youth] thus was wonderful from a stranger. He had never seen him before, was wholly ignorant of his name, his circumstances; he could not be sure that he had not been guilty of some base action which had drawn him into this misfortune and that, instead of a brave and worthy man he had defended, he had not been hazarding his own life for the sake of the worst criminal: a man who, though he called himself a Christian and by that powerful plea entreated his assistance, might yet be banished from his country for some shameful and wicked action. Yet was he attached to him by an impulse which he could not at that time account for. Though this was the first moment of their meeting, already did he love him with a brother's tenderness. (188)

It would, of course, run counter to Haywood's Neoplatonic concept of beauty for the young man to be a villain, but the two most significant features of this passage are that (1) Philidore is powerfully attracted to his new companion's physical beauty in a way he does not readily understand, and that (2) the novel takes immediate pains to diffuse Philidore's love as fraternal rather than potentially homosexual. We should note, for example, how quickly the novel overwrites itself at this point in the narrative: Philidore, looking at a beautiful man, experiences a powerful affective impulse "which he could not at that time account for." This same unaccountable impulse, it turns out, is a kind of spontaneous fraternal affection that allows the two men to bond in a socially acceptable fashion.[19] Is it—let us not say "believable," since that would be to swallow elephants and strain at gnats in terms of Haywood's fiction—but consistent with the romance genre for a hero not to know brotherly love when he feels it? We have a telling precedent for such unaccountability, but it occurs in a decidedly more amorous context. If we recall Placentia's decisive encounter with the disguised Philidore, we find that Haywood describes Placentia's erotic capitulation in an almost identical phrase: "She . . . was once or twice about to call him back; *but something; which at that time she could not account for*, stopped the utterance of her words" (162, my emphasis). Why would Haywood phrase key affective moments, one of heterosexual erotogenesis and one of same-sex "affection," according to the same kind of unaccountability? Do heterosexual love and fraternal love have the same root? Is it not the object of one's love but the intensity of the experience that renders one epistemologically challenged? Is this simply an example of stylistic poverty on Haywood's part? Certainly, Haywood's substitution of "brotherly love" for its more dangerous and inexplicable counterpart is hardly adequate to containing the homoerotic immediacy of Philidore's experience, but in that case, why would Haywood undermine the erotic predictability of what was, after all, only one in a long series of amatory novels?

We can begin to answer these questions only, I believe, if we consider the scene of the Eunuch's castration. Bellamont, to give the Eunuch his Christian name, having been taken as the Bashaw of Liperda's slave when his ship was lost in a storm, falls in love with Arithea, the Bashaw's mistress and "the most loved and beautiful of all the numerous train which crowded his seraglio" (199). During the course of his captivity, Bellamont tries repeatedly to see "the all-dazzling Arithea" and "to proceed to the greatest liberties with her" that his "submissive passion" will allow (205). After his first transgression, the Bashaw's servants beat Bellamont nearly to death; after the second, they deprive him "of all power of ever injuring their lord or any other person in the manner I was about to do and left me nothing but the name of man" (206). Significantly, Haywood remains vague as to exactly what it is that Bellamont loses:

> This beautiful person had been deprived of his manhood, not in the manner as those are whose parents, designing them for the seraglio, in early infancy qualify them for it; but this seemed to have been lately done by the yet recent scar, and consequently the effect of malice. This misfortune, joined with the sight of the picture [of Arithea which Bellamont wears], made Philidore half-assured that love had been the cause of his disgrace but, not doubting that there must be something very remarkable in the story, had his curiosity doubled for the knowledge of it. (192)

What does Bellamont lose? At first the passage seems to suggest that his testicles have been removed in a brutal but routine act of castration performed "not in the manner as those are whose parents, designing them for the seraglio, in early infancy qualify them for it," but "lately done" as "the effect of malice." But the rhetorical force of the term "manhood" makes it equally plausible that what Bellamont has lost is his penis, that phallic signifier most dear to heterosexual masculine identity. For Haywood's purposes, loss of the phallus would be profound, since the phallus bears a tremendous signifying burden, one greater, I think, than anything matched by the female body. While the individual penis never successfully lives up to its task of representing the phallus, it is also true that the phallus and the penis are uniquely prone to a symbolic assimilation that privileges the penis as the site nonpareil of masculine identity. The penis acts as a visual referent guaranteeing that a man is what he claims to be. As Teresa Brennan puts it, "While Lacanians never tire of insisting that the penis and the phallus are not the same thing, and they are right, this visual significance is none the less a point at which penis and phallus converge."[20] If the penis is what allows a man access to his own essential being as something different from a woman, this is precisely the difference Bellamont has lost. Left with "nothing but the name of a man," Bellamont is an empty signifier in a world determined by sexual difference; to speak of him as a man is illogical, since sexual identity, sexual difference, and sexual desire are all correlative in Haywood's gender system. We find, for example, that when Bellamont has recuperated from his wound, the Bashaw further humiliates him by compelling Bellamont to attend Arithea in the seraglio, a fate he once would have embraced ecstatically:

> I recovered, however, and for my greater mortification was ordered to attend the beauties I was now deprived of all possibility of ever possessing. Being qualified for the seraglio, I was compelled to attend there under the direction of that treacherous eunuch who had been entrusted by Arithea to bring me to her and had, as I afterward learned, betrayed us both to the bashaw. (206)

Sadly, daily contact with his former beloved does nothing for Bellamont, since "my sentiments were changed with my condition and, as I had no longer the power of enjoying, had very little of the wish of remaining" (206). Haywood makes it clear that love is ancillary to physical passion; the loss of his manhood also costs Bellamont his devotion to Arithea or to any other beauty who comes his way.[21]

Since it was genital difference that guaranteed Bellamont's masculinity and its hallmark desires, castration effectively frees him from both love and desire. The loss of his sexual difference renders him literally indifferent to the female body and its amatory charms. Such difference also renders him an object of indifference to women. Arithea's last lines to Bellamont urge him to "Fly this barbarous place [the seraglio], O thou once most charming of thy sex, and still valued, though an eunuch" (207). Just as his desire for Arithea dies with his castration, so too her desire for Bellamont disappears. Bellamont no longer "charms" Arithea, even though he does retain a sort of nostalgic "value" for her. In an important sense, then, it matters less whether Bellamont loses the physical penis or whether he suffers testicular castration. Whatever the nature of Bellamont's somatic lack, he symbolically loses the guarantee of his masculinity and can no longer differ reliably from women.

As a consequence, Philidore's attraction to Bellamont *is and is not* homoerotic. To the extent that Bellamont passes for a man, Philidore's desire must be rechanneled as brotherly love so as not to threaten the heterosexual edifice of the novel. But to the extent that Bellamont fails to live up to Haywood's masculine ideal, any attraction to him must remain strictly meaningless—since according to the logic of sexual difference Haywood promulgates, he has no sexuality left to engage the attention of either authentic men or women. What Bellamont does have left is a Platonic and feminizing beauty that Haywood valorizes as his chief attribute: "a young man of a most beautiful aspect" (187); "the lovely stranger" (189); "this beautiful person" (192); "the lovely stranger" (208); "the beautiful Christian eunuch" (227). Bellamont's damaged body makes his beauty all the more striking, and Haywood's particular insistence on the quality aligns Bellamont with the novel's female characters. As he is feminized, and thus as his homoerotic potential diffuses, Bellamont becomes the one individual upon whom sexual desires may safely be displaced. By castrating him, Haywood effectively removes Bellamont from the realm of sexual desires, and by homogenizing the male body toward a female ideal, Haywood rearticulates sexual difference as a controllable category, one that no longer threatens the generic constraints of the amatory novel. As a figure at once neuter and feminine, Bellamont becomes an effective critique of the sexual binarism of English society, since his reduction to a relatively powerless position is one shared by the working-class women in Haywood's audience. What Ann Barr Snitow calls the quotidian "pathological experience of sex difference" becomes in Haywood's novel a means of intervention.[22] This is not to imply that Haywood's female consumers need to be protected from the hard realities of a patriarchal system founded on sexual difference. It is, instead, to recognize the degree to which Haywood exposes the gender conventions of her time by shockingly rewriting the male body as a site of helplessness and indifference. In the traditional seduction novel, women tend to be the object, and men the agent, of suffering and ostracism. But Bellamont's fate tames what Richetti has called "the *libertin*-seducer," the rapacious male appetite that consumes women without remorse.[23] Bellamont's pathetic timorousness before Arithea's "all-dazzling" and dangerously seductive form when whole, and his equally pathetic inertia when faced with the same sexualized female body as a eunuch, recuperate the male body as if it were female, and thus at equal risk in a world of seduction and sexual exploitation. Haywood desexualizes Bellamont so as to reinvest Arithea with a seductive sexual plenitude that—at least momentarily—neutralizes the violence and primacy of patriarchy; when Bellamont fails, patriarchy fails with him.[24] Bellamont is, perhaps, a parody of the violated

virgin, but he is also a nod toward the power of those social conventions which institute sexual difference as the primary constituent of individual identity. At one blow Haywood unmans Bellamont
and successfully renders him a nonperson, sexless and feminized;
and that, in terms of English culture of the 1720s, is a sharp blow
indeed.

FIVE

Reading the Rhetoric of
Sexual Difference in Cleland's
Memoirs of a Woman of Pleasure

In his exploration of early-eighteenth-century Venerean iconography, Douglas Brooks-Davies focuses on John Cleland's *Memoirs of a Woman of Pleasure* as an eroticized romance in which female heterosexuality passes through the marked developmental stages of a specifically feminine mythological narrative:

> Cleland's *Memoirs of a Woman of Pleasure* (1749) is as much romance as pornography. Much of its erotic language and some of its situations derive from Renaissance commonplaces, and so, not surprisingly, it is a novel of Venus. She possesses it, and gives it mythological unity. "Fanny Hill," directly translated, means *mons Veneris*, of course; and the genital descriptions, with their "young tendrils of . . . moss," etc., suggest that we are within the sexual topography of Spenser's Garden of Adonis and related Venerean gardens of pleasure, including Milton's Eden. But Fanny has to learn what, at Mrs. Brown's "college," are known as "the mysteries of Venus," and her initiation follows the familiar

progress from homoerotic to heterosexual, again within a mythological framework.[1]

For Brooks-Davies, Venerean identity is a result of genital specificity: the female genitals are not just part of the mythology of Venus, they are what anchor that mythological identity to a particular place (which in itself condenses the garden and the pubes as an icon of femaleness) and make possible an entire literary tradition. The purpose of Brooks-Davies's essay is to show how the figure of Venus "could be endowed with an almost Renaissance density of moral and psychological meanings" (176) well into the eighteenth century, but, as we see above, Venus and her avatars must first be recognizable as women before they can be recognized as overdetermined signifiers. In other words, before Venus can "possess" and give "mythological unity" to Memoirs, she must first be identified by and with her genitals.

Brooks-Davies's framework, the mythology of Venus and Adonis, invokes a classical male/female binarism to explain the series of sexual episodes in which Fanny takes part, and his essay clearly relates Fanny's sexual identity to an unambiguously progressive narrative of sexual initiation in which Fanny's increasingly sublime sexual encounters move purposively towards a reunion with her beautiful male lover, Charles. Brooks-Davies gives us four specific instances of female sexuality to illustrate this Venerean progression: three prostitutes, Louisa, Polly, and Phoebe, represent opposite end points on the line that Fanny as the fourth example traces in her search for Charles, with Louisa and Polly embodying an instinctual and "mature" desire for men, and Phoebe representing a permanently "immature" interest in lesbian sexuality. "Louisa 'instinctively' knows, however, that 'man alone' will be her cure" for unrequited sexual desire; Polly, paired with her Genoese lover "has found her complement," while "Phoebe appears not to need one" (185). Fanny "meets hers immediately" after seeing Polly correctly paired off and thus, according to Brooks-Davies's reading, fulfills the hetero-sexual promise of her early desires.[2]

Brooks-Davies's essay is itself part of a decade-long reconsideration of male and female sexuality in *Memoirs of a Woman of Pleasure* that has produced critiques of Cleland's ventriloquization of female subjects, of the power of the phallus to support its symbolic burden, and of the novel's ability adequately to represent the disruptive force of homosexuality within and for a homophobic society. Indeed, his essay is contemporary with what is arguably the best-known gender critique of Cleland, Nancy Miller's "'I's' in Drag," which contends that "Cleland's cheerful, even comic pornography in the final analysis supports the prerogatives of both class and masculinity."[3] Miller hypothesizes that

> the founding contract of the novel as it functions in the phallocentric (heterosexual) economies of representation is homoerotic: "woman" is the legal fiction, the present absence that allows the male bond of privilege and authority to constitute itself within the laws of proper circulation. (49)

Miller also argues that

> the erotics of female impersonation is a mirroring not of female desire but of a phallic pride of place, a wish-fulfillment that ultimately translates into structures of masculine dominance and authority. (54)

Miller's reading of a totalizing *masculine* fantasy aligns her essay with that of Brooks-Davies on the critical continuum: if Brooks-Davies sees *Woman of Pleasure* as the emergence of a purposive female heterosexuality patterned on the dominant cultural model of classical mythology, Miller sees the novel as a usurpation of female identity by a masculinity organized around and safeguarded by the phallus, but what both essays hold in common is the relative stability of the categories "male" and "female," especially as those categories refer to bodies in Cleland's novel.[4] Miller's general project is, after all, a critique of reading practices that overlook gender as an interpretive issue, and her particular project in "'I's' in Drag" is to question the position of an identifiably masculine subjectivity in the formation of the eighteenth-century novel:

> Although it has become a critical commonplace to claim that the eighteenth-century novel evolved under the sign of "woman"—hypostatized in feminocentric fables consumed by a female reading public—what seems less clear is the ideological content of the masculine investment in such an economy. More specifically, what secondary gains accrue to a male writer who supplies first-person feminine fictions—translations, as it were—within this system of production? (49)

Miller's argument requires this easy alignment of masculinity with male bodies, primarily because her idea of drag necessitates a fundamental mispairing of discrete genital and gendered identities to work. Miller disputes critical exegeses that "disembody the problematics of production" (48); her own reading makes production a "bodily" process, but at the expense of rigidly associating genital identity with categories of cultural identity. As a consequence, "gender" as a reading category in Miller's own essay ultimately refers to a simple "reimbodiment" of sexual difference as genital difference. In effect, Miller's desire to theorize a less restricted female subjectivity only liberates the bearer of a particularly female genital while at the same time perniciously equating social constructions of masculinity with the male body.

More recent criticism in this vein has attempted, not always

successfully, to displace this stable categorical opposition by reading *Memoirs*'s scenes of homosexual intercourse against their heterosexual counterparts. Kevin Kopelson argues, for instance, that

> For Fanny, the significance of sexual intercourse depends
> upon the confluence, correspondence, and stability of two
> oppositions: sexual difference (male/female) and gender dif-
> ference (phallic penetration/phallic reception). The lesbian
> activity in *Fanny Hill* does not transcend significance: it
> violates sexual difference, but, because it does not involve
> phallic penetration, respects gender difference. Even the
> pederastic adventure signifies because Emily, after all, is
> "really" a girl. Homosexual sodomy, however, does not re-
> spect the coding of phallic penetration as "male" and phal-
> lic receptivity as "female," and consequently explodes the
> binary "bottom or groundwork" of sexual signification. It
> is erotically, transgressively, transcendently exempt from
> meaning.[5]

Exempt from meaning for whom, though? Certainly not for
Mrs. Cole, the genteel madam of Fanny's last brothel, who does
not, as Kopelson thinks, transcend sexual signification when she
describes the sodomites as "unsexed male misses."[6] Homosexuality
may indeed disturb Mrs. Cole's notions of heterosexual propriety
and thus render the sodomites "unsexed" in terms of her interpretive conventions, but since these sodomitical male bodies remain
readable as "male misses" even while they "transgress" or "transcend" heterosexual meaning, they preserve the categorical attributes
of Cleland's heterosexual system even as they "misdirect" their
sexual energies. Conversely, Kopelson's impoverished reading of
lesbian sexuality suggests that lesbians are somehow incapable of
traversing the heterosexual differential of "phallic penetration/
phallic reception" as lesbians. Presumably, this is because lesbians

in *Memoirs*, lacking the phallus, cannot evade what Kopelson calls "the dominant structural paradigm of vaginal intercourse" (176) in the same way that privileged male homosexuals can. The lesbians in Cleland's text have tongues, hands, fingers, and imaginations, but unfortunately no penises. Kopelson argues in essence that a vagina does not always have to be a vagina, as in the case of male homosexual copulation, but his reading of *Memoirs* nevertheless insists that a penis always has to be a penis. In this instance, it is not Cleland's novel that relegates lesbian sexuality to the realm of the heterosexual binarism, but Kopelson's reading, insofar as Kopelson turns the "gender difference" of phallic penetration and reception into a mark of sexual distinction that reassuringly differentiates homosexual men from lesbians. Kopelson's attempt to produce a gay and revisionary reading of male sodomy is certainly worthwhile as far as it goes, but the exclusionary and rhapsodic subjectivity he discovers is hardly consistent with the understanding of and identification with "Otherness" he describes at the end of his essay.[7]

It is this critical reinscription of organically grounded heterosexual difference common to *Memoirs of a Woman of Pleasure* and to so many of its readings that prompts me to ask just how effectively the male and female organs constitute unquestioned referents for sexual identity, and how that referential function regulates the complementarity of Cleland's two sexes. In all of the criticism I have cited, sexual difference sooner or later means reliable genital difference, so that male and female bodies, regardless of the context in which they occur, remain readable as physically dissimilar and therefore socially and significatively distinct. The consequence of this sort of reading is that whether or not the difference between male and female becomes a mark of subjection or of complementarity, the mark itself remains apparent and even natural to the point that it ceases to be an object of critical attention in itself.[8] In this chapter, I suggest that the function of genital reference in *Memoirs of a Woman of Pleasure*, so often naturalized and obscured as "sexual difference" both in the novel and in its attendant criticism, itself actively destabilizes any static notion of sexual identity, whether that identity is a natural heterosexual one or a perverse expression of homosexuality or lesbianism. I argue that Clelandian bodies do not simply present themselves in transparently sexual situations. They are, rather, part of a complex and problematically executed system of representation in which Cleland attempts to use genital reference to produce apparently natural male and female referents as a strategy for the stabilization of the very identities his novel is supposed merely to describe. Heterosexuality and homosexuality in *Memoirs* are not, in other words, the general result of particular genital sex acts, but of particular reading acts.[9]

Natural sexuality in Cleland's writing presents itself as the predictable operation of sexual difference. Male and female bodies simultaneously refer to each other differentially to produce the meaning of bodily sexuality and invoke each other as complementary opposites. This invocation of the corresponding sex makes heterosexual difference the principal concept in Cleland's hierarchy of sexual relations, and the strongest evidence for the totalizing effect of this natural heterosexual complementarity is the body itself. Cleland repeatedly represents the body, and especially the male body, as a symbol of the sexual promise heterosexual intercourse realizes. A clear example of this promise can be found in Cleland's 1751 novel, *Memoirs of a Coxcomb*, which Cleland may have published as an attempt to reintroduce himself to a London reading public outraged over the explicit sexual contents of *Memoirs of a Woman of Pleasure*.[10] *Memoirs of a Coxcomb*, as William Epstein has noted, serves roughly as a sequel to *Memoirs of a Woman of Pleasure*.[11] It envisions the career of an aristocratic young libertine whose sexual confessions, like Fanny's, make up the bulk of the novel. *Coxcomb* differs significantly from *Memoirs of a Woman of Pleasure*, though, in terms of the social and economic codes of conduct to which its

hero conforms: Sir William Delamore, the young libertine, is heir
to two fine English estates and thus begins his sexual career in a
position of social authority that Fanny only approximates at the end
of her story. Like *Memoirs of a Woman of Pleasure*, however,
Delamore's narrative portrays heterosexual attraction as the self-
evident meaning of a bodily sexuality that erupts into the world of
the social:

> My blood now boiling in my veins, began to make me
> feel the ferment of desire for objects far more interesting
> than horses and dogs. And a robust, healthy constitution,
> manifest in the glow of a fresh complexion, and vigorous
> well-proportioned limbs, gave me those warnings of my rip-
> ening manhood, and its favourite destination, by which
> nature prevents all instruction, and suggests the use of those
> things that most engage our attention, without putting us
> to the blush of asking silly questions. I had not indeed waited
> till then for the dawn of certain desires, and wishes: but
> besides their being only imperfect ones, and crudities of over-
> tender youth, my hours, and opportunities had been all so
> confined either to my studies, exercises, boyish amusements,
> or my aunt's fondness for my being as little out of her sight
> as possible; that I had not the least room to encourage such
> ideas, or give them hope enough to live upon. Accordingly
> they generally died away of themselves, like a faint breeze
> that had just blown enough to ruffle the surface of my imagi-
> nation, for a few instants, and flattened into a calm again.
> But now, those transient desires inspired by this rising pas-
> sion, began to take a more settled hold of my imagination,
> and to grow into such tender pantings, such an eagerness of
> wishes, as quite overcame, and engrossed me intirely.
> Woman it was, that I may say, I instinctively knew, was
> wanting to my happiness; but I had as yet no determined

object in that sex, but yearned, and looked out for one every where. (6–7)[12]

Two points are immediately apparent from this passage. First, Delamore's sexuality develops over time, so that at a particular moment it becomes appropriate to speak of him as sexually mature, but sexuality, and specifically male sexuality per se, is somehow always "there" in his body. The "transient desires" of "over-tender youth" that die away from lack of a proper object or opportunity consequently refer to the natural and perpetually present sexuality of which they are a temporal intimation. Second, Delamore's passion is not coextensive with his conscious self, since his "boiling blood" has to make him "feel the ferment of desire for objects far more interesting than horses and dogs." Rather, Cleland figures sexual desire as an expression of the promise Delamore's body incarnates as a sign of its own naturalness and something Delamore's mediating consciousness must read off of his own body. "A robust, healthy constitution, manifest in the glow of a fresh complexion, and vigorous well-proportioned limbs" suggests a perfect fit between the body as signifier and sexuality as signified, since Delamore's body serves as the outward sign for an inward, and therefore natural, desire. Delamore's limbs, for instance, can be well proportioned only insofar as the idea of "proportion" presupposes a correct relation between Delamore's body and the world around it, but the "correctness" of that relation is itself a function of Delamore's essential manhood; "correct proportion" is consequently a corollary of his immanent heterosexuality, and both "correctness" and "proportion" are thus recuperated as essential expressions of Delamore's sexuality, rather than as contingent relations between "body" and "context." As "warnings of my ripening manhood, and its favourite destination," Delamore's limbs serve as a sign of the already interior heterosexual knowledge "by which nature prevents all instruction, and suggests the use of those things that most engage our attention."

Delamore's body *is* knowledge, both of essential sexual being and of that being's performative expression; here, the male body indicates its true nature as well as its natural object without ever putting Delamore as subject in need of social discourse and "the blush of asking silly questions." Delamore's male heterosexuality is, as its expression as prior knowledge indicates, not simply one innate characteristic of his being, but the dominant characteristic defining his identity.

This ideology of innate heterosexuality appears repeatedly in *Memoirs of a Coxcomb*. At one point, Delamore explains his desirability to women in terms of the masculine promise he both embodies and enacts:

> All vanity apart, I was at that time certainly not without pretensions to please. I had at least the merit, of a fair ruddy complexion, shapely stature, *promising strength of limbs*, and all the native attendants of a healthy, untainted youth; I was at that nice point in short, when imminent manhood brings on essential maturity for action, without abating any thing of the smooth of youth, or of those tender bloomy graces, which endear that age to those women especially who have rather delicate than craving appetites. (82, my emphasis)

Strangely, Delamore's "pretensions to please" have nothing to do with his ability to please, since the claim here is that he must please women whether or not his vanity prompts him intentionally to do so. The correlative of Delamore's particular kind of manhood, "a healthy, untainted youth" ornamented by "those tender bloomy graces," is its essential attractiveness to those constituted to be attracted to it (women of certain appetites). The more general category of "manhood," however, always applies to Delamore and always places him on a trajectory towards women. Delamore's "imminent manhood" might seem to undermine the status of his sexual identity because it implies a time before full male sexuality and thus before full male subjectivity, but the *promise* of manhood is something Delamore's body perpetually displays as a sign of his true self. The "nice point" at which Delamore finds himself sexually is a symbol of his liminal sexual identity: he is man and boy, capable of acting without having acted, pure potential. Male sexual maturity is, for him, achieved by the revelation of his potential for sexual maturity in a significative circle where the body and those signs derived from it continually fold back upon each other. Delamore's "promising strength of limbs," for example, is part of his sexual desirability, but this strength can be sexual only because everything about his body is (hetero)sexualized and desirable the moment it can be seen as representative of his essential manhood. Interiority and exteriority are, for him, mutually referential because the body is never itself simply sexual without reference to some interior quality of desire that makes the "sexual" identifiable, and desire is nothing more than the proper operation of Delamore's male body. What Delamore *is* (a man) remains indistinguishable from what he *does* (he acts), in a way making performativity a token of essence, so that the promise of his heterosexual destiny foregrounds that very performativity in the promise itself and guarantees male identity regardless of Delamore's temporal ability to execute the promise he represents. Genital reference as a sign of complementary sexual difference has here been dispersed throughout Delamore's phallic "limbs" and has become their meaning to the degree that "the use of those things that most engage our attention" (6) is never questionable, either by Delamore or by his partners.

Fanny, too, gives promise of the sex she is and in which she will engage, but the language she uses to recall her young body and its sexual potential is more open-ended than Delamore's. Fanny remembers her first sexual contact with the prostitute, Phoebe, as a series of original sensations:

> I lay then all tame and passive as she could wish, whilst
> her freedom, raised no other emotion but those of a strange,
> and till then unfelt pleasure: every part of me was open,
> and exposed to the licentious courses of her hands, which
> like a lambent fire ran over my whole body, and thaw'd all
> coldness as they went. (11)

Fanny's body, like Delamore's, becomes the principal locus for bodily
knowledge, but unlike Delamore, Fanny comes to know about her
sexuality through Phoebe's intervention. Fanny now understands
that "every part of me was open," and she knows what that open-
ness feels like, but this knowledge is process-oriented (that is, toward
the production of pleasure), whereas Delamore's bodily knowledge
is a static embodiment of his masculine potential. This first bodily
pleasure, which it would make sense to call sexual even though
Fanny later rejects it as parodic of heterosexual intercourse and
thus inferior,[13] leads immediately to a description of the body that
has been thus aroused:

> My breasts, if it is not too bold a figure to call so, two
> hard, firm, rising hillocs, that just began to shew themselves,
> or signify any thing to the touch, employ'd and amused her
> hands a while, till slipping down lower, over a smooth track,
> she could just feel the soft, silky down that had but a few
> months before put forth, and garnish'd the mount-pleasant
> of those parts, and promised to spread a grateful shelter
> over the sweet seat of the most exquisite sensation, and
> which had been, till that instant, the seat of the most insen-
> sible innocence. (11)

Fanny's female sexuality is, for the moment, a much less determi-
nate kind of identity than the one Cleland imagines for Delamore,
in part because her body expresses its femininity less imminently

than his body expresses its masculinity. Since her breasts have just begun "to shew themselves, or signify any thing to the touch," they are less able to pose as signs of her innate femaleness in the way Delamore's well-proportioned limbs can stand in for his maleness. Indeed, her body seems less to bear its sexuality as a reification of identity than it does to enact a sexual identity even as Fanny relates her experiences to us. Phoebe's touch transforms a "seat of the most insensible innocence" into one of "the most exquisite sensation" without at the same time necessarily exciting anything essentially feminine or purposive in Fanny or in her new-found sexuality. Fanny submits to Phoebe's caresses in the first place because "it might be the *London* way to express" "pure kindness" (10), and when Phoebe excites Fanny's "sweet seat," all Fanny feels is pleasure. Unlike Delamore, she does not intuitively understand that "Man it was, that I may say, I instinctively knew, was wanting to my happiness," but she also does not understand that her encounter with Phoebe can be sexual in its own right.[14] Cleland thus desexualizes Fanny's encounter with Phoebe by identifying Phoebe with the contingencies of culture (specifically, London culture) rather than with the teleology of female sexuality.

What Fanny does understand, and what is most natural about her encounter with Phoebe, is that her once "insensible" genitals have been irrevocably sensitized to an intense and, as it turns out, determinative pleasure. As Phoebe's finger penetrates her, Fanny switches to the erotic present tense that she also uses when penetrated by her more obviously phallic male partners:[15]

But not contented with these outer-posts, she now attempts the main-spot, and began to twitch, to insinuate, and at length to force an introduction of a finger into the quick itself, in such a manner, that had she not proceeded by insensible gradations, that enflamed me beyond the power of modesty to oppose its resistance to their progress, I should

have jump'd out of bed, and cried out for help against such
strange assaults.

Instead of which, her lascivious touches had lighted up
a new fire that wanton'd through all my veins, but fix'd
with violence in that center appointed them by nature, where
the first strange hands were now busied in feeling, squeez-
ing, compressing the lips, then opening them again, with a
finger between, till an Oh! express'd her hurting me, where
the narrowness of the unbroken passage refused it entrance
to any depth. (11, my emphasis)

Fanny's body, like other sexual bodies, encloses a performative promise of sexuality to be realized, since the "narrowness of the unbroken passage" reminds us that passages must be passed through and
to fulfill this promise, Fanny's "passage" must submit itself to the
violence of its own potential. This site could, for all intents and
purposes, be read as Fanny's anus if it were not for this "fire" that
Phoebe lights and that will burn with a periodic and natural intensity throughout the rest of the novel. The text suggests, first, that
Phoebe penetrates Fanny at the point where Fanny is most alive, or
"quick," and, second, that Phoebe's transformative penetration
consequently brings her into contact with Fanny's unmediated self;
Phoebe's "strange assaults" thus activate whatever is most authentic about Fanny by introducing Fanny to the sexual pleasure her
body affords. The effect of this introduction to herself, though, is
to suspend Fanny's mediating subjectivity at precisely the moment
it becomes most self-apparent:

For my part, I was transported, confused, and out of
myself: Feelings so new were too much for me; my heated
and alarm'd senses were in a tumult that robb'd me of all
liberty of thought; tears of pleasure gush'd from my eyes, and
somewhat assuaged the fire that rag'd all over me. (11–12)

Ironically, Fanny consummates the moment in which she becomes most aware of her newfound potential as a female body with a symbolic ejaculation of soothing tears and so reaffirms the unstable character of the gender identity she is in the process of assuming. Peter Sabor comments in his explanatory notes that "Cleland shared the prevalent eighteenth-century view that women as well as men ejaculated with orgasm" (196), so female ejaculation as such is less the issue here than Fanny's almost masturbatory ability to "somewhat assuage" the fire of her own desire without a man's physical presence or action.

As we have seen, Cleland's determinedly euphemistic treatment of Fanny's body makes it difficult to tell whether or not this "seat" is an anus or a vagina, but if we compare Fanny's experience to a later scene when the prostitute, Emily, encounters a sodomitically minded "gentleman in a very handsome domino" (154), we can see that, given a choice, one of the two openings receives preferential treatment:

> for now, whether the impression of so great a beauty had even made him forgive her, her sex, or whether her appearance or figure in that dress still humour'd his first illusion, he recover'd by degrees a good part of his first warmth, and keeping *Emily* with her breeches still unbuttoned, stript them down to her knees, and gently impelling her to lean down, with her face against the bedside, placed her so, that the double-way between the double rising behind, presented the choice fair to him, and he was so fiercely set on a misdirection, as to give the girl no small alarms for fear of loosing a maiden-head she had not dreamt of. . . . (155)

Emily soon manages, though, to drive her recalcitrant partner "at length into the right road," where the male penis and an appropriate female opening produce the usual results. Though Cleland never

specifies what that opening is, the passage does posit the possibility
of "mis-directing" those parts "so admirably fitted for each other"
(see below), and while this misdirection strongly implies the nonnecessity of heterosexual intercourse, it just as strongly supposes
that the female body does have right and wrong orifices that may
take part in sexual intercourse. The effect of this ambiguity is to
center proper male sexual attention on the female body as an indeterminate pleasurable site to which the specificity of genital reference no longer strictly applies.

This problem with determining the correct site of female sexual
pleasure explains Cleland's insistence that "fire" in the "center appointed by nature" is the essential sign of female heterosexuality in
Memoirs. Fanny first feels this sort of burning when she watches
Mrs. Brown, the loathsome old brothel-keeper, have intercourse
with her handsome retainer, a "tall, brawny, young horse-grenadier, moulded in the *Hercules*-stile" (24). Watching from her
mistress's "dark closet," Fanny sees an erect penis for the first time:

> Her sturdy stallion had now unbutton'd, and produced
> naked, stiff, and erect, that wonderful machine, which I
> had never seen before, and which, for the interest my own
> seat of pleasure began to take furiously in it, I star'd at with
> all the eyes I had: however my senses were too much flur-
> ried, too much concenter'd in that now burning spot of mine,
> to observe any thing more than in general the make and
> turn of that instrument, from which the instinct of nature,
> yet more than all I had heard of it, now strongly informed
> me, I was to expect that supreme pleasure which she has
> placed in the meeting of those parts so admirably fitted for
> each other. (25)

Fanny's previous sexual experience with Phoebe also incites a pleasurable burning that Fanny has to extinguish with "tears of pleasure"

(12), but the sensations Phoebe produces on Fanny's body, and especially in her "center" or "quick," suggest no reciprocal relation between the object and agent of stimulation. Fanny carefully records that Phoebe "raised no other emotion" (11) than pleasure, while Fanny now feels the burning discomfort of expectation in relation to the horse-grenadier. Here, though, Cleland explicitly relates the male penis to Fanny's sensations and to the "seat" of her pleasure so that the male and female sites are naturally and "admirably fitted for each other." The novel's last scene of heterosexual intercourse finds Fanny and Charles coupled so complementarily that Fanny can only recall the moment of penetration in superlatives. Finally reunited with Charles, Fanny cannot "help feeling the stiff stake that had been adorned with the trophies of my despoiled virginity, bearing hard and inflexible against one of my thighs" (182), and she portrays her own reaction to "that favourite piece of manhood" in terms of a categorical address to her audience: "Nothing can be dearer to the touch, or can affect it with a more delicious sensation" (183). Her particular response to Charles's "piece of manhood" is very much a part of the novel's ideology of complementarity:

> And now, at its mightiest point of stiffness, it felt to me something so subduing, so active, so solid, and agreeable that I know not what name to gives its singular impression; but the sentiment of consciousness of its belonging to my supremely beloved youth, gave me so pleasing an agitation, and work'd so strongly on my soul, that it sent all its sensitive spirits to that organ of bliss in me, dedicated to its reception: there concentering to a point, like rays in a burning-glass, they glow'd, they burnt with the intensest heat. . . . (183)

Ideally, this scene gives us Fanny's heterosexual body at its most unmediated and self-representative. The male organ, "so subduing, so active, so solid," finds its counterpart in the female "organ of bliss . . . dedicated to its reception," and the result is a sensory plenitude in which touch, taste, sight, and hearing all express the same intense and unmediated pleasure: Fanny finds herself "in touch at once with the instrument of pleasure, and the great-seal of love"; she feels and hears herself panting with "so exquisitely keen an appetite for the imminent enjoyment, that I was even sick with desire" (183); she finds that "the sight of my idolized youth, was, alone from the ardour with which I had wish'd for it, without other circumstance, a pleasure to die for" (182); in short, "the sense of his glowing body in naked touch with mine, took all power over my thoughts out of my own disposal, and deliver'd up every faculty of my soul to the sensiblest of joys" (182). Thought as a mediating influence between the body and the conscious subject must surrender itself to the immediacy of heterosexual intercourse, which serves here as the most naturally self-representative experience complementary male and female bodies may have.[16] We may wonder, though, if Fanny's failure to "name" the "singular impression" that Charles's "peculiar scepter-member" (183) makes on her is simply an indication of language's inability to do justice to the transcendent immediacy of natural heterosexual intercourse, or if Fanny herself lacks the language necessary to constitute as comprehensible the impression Charles's organ makes on her. If the former, language is inherently inadequate to the immediacy of complementary heterosexual difference as that difference culminates in its purposive resolution. If the latter, then the self-evident truth of heterosexual complementarity itself comes into question, since the one thing Fanny should be able to name is the singularity of the difference between herself and her lover.

Fanny's lover, Charles, also exhibits an innate and complementary desirability that makes him the proper object of Fanny's interest. Like Delamore, Charles signifies an ideal masculinity that finds its representation and its expression in his body, but unlike the subject of Delamore's autobiographical narrative, Charles exists for the reader only as a function of Fanny's mediating recollections. Since the hallmark of Clelandian masculinity is its self-present immediacy as and in itself, such mediation might be fatal to Cleland's ideology of essential manhood if Fanny did not insist on the reality of Charles's presence even across the gulf of recollection.[17] By feeling and writing simultaneously, Fanny appears to bridge the gap between herself and the object of her desire:

> Oh! could I paint his figure as I see it now still present to my transported imagination! a whole length of an all-perfect manly beauty in full view. Think of a face without a fault, glowing with all the opening bloom, and vernal freshness of an age, in which beauty is of either sex, and which the first down over his upper-lip scarce began to distinguish. (44)

Fanny's recollection subtly but carefully distinguishes between the nude body present to her memory and the body that her memoirs make present to us. The Charles fully present to her "transported imagination" is complete, completely masculine, and perfectly beautiful in a manner that yokes these characteristics together and implies a descriptive interchangeability among them. The Charles she invokes through her implied address to the reader is also young and beautiful, but youth and beauty here cannot by themselves bear the burden of masculine signification, since "beauty is of either sex," and sexual difference requires a more potent signifier. Masculinity here, rather than being self-apparent as Charles's masculinity is to Fanny, must be actively read off this body in the form of its downy upper lip, a sign that, as its acknowledged near illegibility indicates, can "scarce [begin] to distinguish" the difference giving rise to heterosexual identity.

Charles, like Delamore, combines the rosy sexual ambiguity of youth with what the novel defines as explicitly masculine attributes, but since *Memoirs of a Woman of Pleasure* deals with explicitness in ways *Memoirs of a Coxcomb* cannot, Fanny has the narrative leisure to indulge in a close reading of her lover's body that Delamore's self-revelations can only hint at. Fanny lingers over Charles, "devouring" "his naked charms" (44) and giving his body precedence while at the same time opening that body to the destabilizing influence of interpretation. Fanny presents us with

> a neck exquisitely turn'd, grac'd behind and on the sides with his hair playing freely in natural ringlets, [which] connected his head to a body of the most perfect form, and of the most vigorous contexture, in which all the strength of manhood was conceal'd and soften'd to appearance, by the delicacy of his complexion, the smoothness of his skin, and the plumpness of his flesh. (44)

Is this "conceal'd and soften'd" masculinity feminized, or simply made different from both the female body and the mature male body by Fanny's rhetoric of youthful delicacy? The "plumpness" of Charles's body, which later includes "the rounding swell of the hips . . . where the skin, sleek, smooth, and dazzling white, burnishes on the stretch over firm, plump-ripe flesh" (44), embeds a performative promise like the promise of Delamore's well-proportioned physique. Where, though, Delamore's body guaranteed masculinity as a form of potential kinetic energy that is present and real, but unrealized, the metaphors surrounding Charles are of a different nature. We can, with Fanny, actually see Charles naked and can thus confirm as self-evident fact the genital nature of his difference from women. The organic, rosy ripeness of his flesh suggests that Charles's body (and the sexuality for which that body acts as agent and referent) is fully natural in the same way that roses and ripe fruit are natural, which is to say unintended, unconscious, and intuitively noncultural. Fanny's description of Charles enacts his masculinity as potential, but as potential dependent not so much on innate desire, as in Delamore's case, as on the self-apparent and organically symbolized naturalness of the naked male body. Charles's "ripeness," as with Delamore's "proportion," seems to be a state of being capable of satisfying in itself, but only because it presupposes some proper and unmotivated relation between essence and agency.

Charles's young body displays "all the strength of manhood," but because we are dealing with this body as a readable surface, the marks of Charles's "manhood" and the marks of his youth do not always coincide neatly. Fanny tells us, for instance, that

> The parting of the double ruby-pout of his lips, seem'd to exhale an air sweeter and purer than what it drew in: Ah! what violence did it not cost me to refrain the so tempted kiss? (44)

Charles's youthful, beautiful mouth recalls another pair of lips. The first chance Fanny has to kiss a man comes when the repulsive and elderly Mr. Crofts stupefies and nearly rapes her in her apartment at Mrs. Brown's house:

> But long I was not suffered to remain in this state of stupefaction: the monster squatted down by me on the settee, and without farther ceremony, or preamble, flings his arms about my neck, and drawing me pretty forcibly towards him, oblig'd me to receive, in spite of my struggles to disengage from him, his pestilential kisses, which quite overcame me. . . . (18)

Mr. Crofts's diseased kisses become all the more awful if we remember the picture of him that Fanny invites us to imagine:

> Imagine to yourself, a man rather past threescore, short and ill made, with a yellow cadaverous hue, great goggling

eyes, that stared as if he was strangled; an out-mouth from two more properly tushes than teeth, livid lips, and a breath like a jakes; then he had a peculiar ghastliness in his grin, that made him perfectly frightful, if not dangerous to women with child; yet made as he was thus in mock of man, he was so blind to his own staring deformities, as to think himself born for pleasing, and that no woman could see him with impunity. . . . (15)

Charles's young mouth "imprints" Fanny with "burning rapture-kisses, which darted a flame to my heart" (45); Mr. Crofts can only "glew" "his lips to mine with an ardour which his figure had not at all disposed me to thank him for" (15). Charles and Mr. Crofts are both men, at least insofar as they both differ from Fanny, but sexual difference is much less significant here than the difference between youth and age. Mr. Crofts's deathly cadaverousness contrasts sharply with Charles's "ripe" beauty; the juxtaposition of age and beauty is thus doubly significant. Mr. Crofts's body successfully represents its own hideousness as a form of sexual inadequacy inseparable from the inadequacies of age, but more importantly, its ugliness differentiates it starkly from the youthful beauty Charles and Fanny share. This similarity suggests that the primary heterosexual difference that structures the ideal sexual pleasure Fanny and Charles experience is itself structured by an internal hierarchy of other oppositions, since mere genital dissimilarity is not by itself enough to satisfy the requirements of a truly sexual scene.

By using the same language to describe both herself and Charles, Fanny refigures herself and her lover according to a logic of rhetorical similarity that renders the two of them remarkably "homo" sexual. At one point, she recalls that her hair "was a glossy auburn, and as soft as silk, flowing down my neck, in natural buckles, and did not a little set off the whiteness of a smooth skin." Her face "was rather too ruddy, though its features were delicate," and her teeth, "which I ever carefully preserv'd, were small, even, and white" (14). Charles shares "the delicacy of his complexion, the smoothness of his skin" (44) with Fanny, and, like her, his white skin sets off the ruddiness of his youth and health. This healthy blush illuminates Fanny's memory of her first sight of Charles:

> Figure to yourself, *Madam*, a fair stripling, between eighteen and nineteen, with his head reclin'd on one of the sides of the chair, his hair in disorder'd curls, irregularly shading a face, on which all the roseate bloom of youth, and all the manly graces conspired to fix my eyes and heart. Even the languor and paleness of his face, in which the momentary triumph of the lilly over the rose, was owing to the excess of the night, gave an inexpressible sweetness to the finest features imaginable. . . . (34–35)

The "roseate bloom of youth" seems here something superadded to, even detachable from, "all the manly graces," so that "beauty" and "manliness" cease to be coextensive terms and instead serve as allied but distinguishable attributes of a body in which beauty and youth now merge.

Charles's "roseate" whiteness recurs in relation to every part of his body. After doting on "his fore-head, which was high, perfectly white and smooth; then a pair of vermillion lips, pouting, and swelling to the touch, as if a bee had freshly stung them" (35), Fanny's gaze moves further on:

> But on seeing his shirt collar unbutton'd, and a bosom whiter than a drift of snow, the pleasure of considering it could not bribe me to lengthen it at the hazard of a health that began to be my life's concern. . . . (35)

Charles's bosom returns in Fanny's most extensive scene of voyeurism:

> The plat-form of his snow-white bosom, that was laid
> out in a manly proportion, presented on the vermillion
> summet of each pap, the idea of a rose about to blow. (44)[18]

Again, masculinity is metonymically allied with figures of organic
beauty: Fanny likens Charles's nipples to "a rose about to blow,"
but since this metonymy only associates the male body with an
organic correlative without asserting a figural equality, the relation
between manliness and organicism remains, at best, strategic. Each
"vermillion summet," after all, only props up an "idea" of its own
roselike representation without necessarily becoming that representation. Charles's kind of masculinity seems thus to be one where
manly form contains and orders an organic, sexually indeterminate content while still contrasting recognizably with that content.
If Delamore's masculinity emanates from within himself, Charles's
masculinity is more a function of the borders and surfaces of his
body that give "proportion" its meaning as a sign of male identity.

The "manly proportion" of Charles's pale chest itself pales in
comparison to "that terrible spit-fire machine" which serves as the
culmination of Charles's masculine characteristics, and on which
Fanny dwells longest in her catalogue of Charles's attributes.[19] This
is the second "wonderful machine" Fanny has seen, and the first
she has ever had the opportunity to examine.[20] In its flaccid state,
Charles's penis is part of the organic imagery constituting his body.
Fanny tells us to

> but behold it now! crestfall'n, reclining its half-capt ver-
> million head over one of his thighs, quiet, pliant, and to all
> appearance incapable of the mischiefs and cruelty it had
> committed. The beautiful growth of the hair, in short and

soft curls round its root, its whiteness, branch'd veins, the supple softness of the shaft, as it lay foreshorten'd roll'd and shrunk up into a squob thickness, languid, and born up from between the thighs, by its globular appendage, that wondrous treasure-bag of nature's sweets, which rivell'd round, and purs'd up in the only wrinkles that are known to please, perfected the prospect. . . . (45)

Carol Houlihan Flynn has written that the first flaccid penis of Fanny's memoirs (the horse-grenadier's), instead of inspiring awe at phallic potential, leaves an impression of phallic impotence:

But even in this first primal siting of the phallus, not only its power but its pathos manifests itself. After his first ejaculation, the magnificent grenadier shrinks, [like Charles] his "capital part" "now crest-fallen, or just faintly lifting its head." This engrossing scene that so stirs Fanny's most sublime passions must also stir in the reader a certain sense of the ridiculous.[21]

I want to argue that what Flynn identifies as the pathos of the phallus, its ridiculousness in the face of desire for it, is really a function of the internal oppositions structuring the penis as privileged sign of male identity. Insofar as it conforms to the imagery of organic youth, Charles's penis can be meaningfully comprehended in organic terms. It is "white," with "branch'd veins" like a tree; its "half-capt vermillion head" recalls the "vermillion summet of each pap" that almost blossoms like a rose; it is even "born up from between the thighs" like an infant, while "its globular appendage" holds "nature's sweets." All in all, this penis forms "the most interesting moving picture in nature, and surely infinitely superior to those nudities furnish'd by the painters, statuaries, or any art" (45), despite the fact that Charles's body is a surface that "the touch could not rest upon, but slid over as on the surface of the most polish'd ivory" (44). Fanny ends her viewing with a pertinent aesthetic judgment on the difference between natural penises and their artistic imitations in paint or marble,

> which are purchas'd at immense prices, whilst the sight of them in actual life is scarce sovereignly tasted by any but the few whom nature has endowed with a fire of imagination, warmly pointed by a truth of judgment to the spring-head, the originals of beauty of nature's unequall'd composition, above all the imitations of art, or the reach of wealth to pay their price. (45)

This ecstatic and rather incoherent statement of aesthetic principle marks a penile apotheosis, because it is here that Charles's "natural" penis, and the masculinity for which it stands, is most clearly and intentionally set off from the cultural world of artifice and artistic contrivance.[22] Fanny seems to be saying that representations of the penis and testicles are enjoyed most by those "whom nature has endowed with a fire of imagination," but she also seems to be saying that this imagination must be guided or "warmly pointed by a truth of judgment to the spring-head" of that desire, the organic male genital. She thus portrays Charles's naturally beautiful penis as the ideal to which artistic representations both aspire and refer, but implicit in her statement is the idea that aesthetic "judgment" must somehow turn the natural imagination that desires the penis toward that desire's already natural object, and even if this desire results from the "truth of judgment," the immediacy of natural heterosexual desire is interrupted by such a need to judge before desiring.

Charles's penis is also, as we have seen, described in recurrent mechanical images that Cleland intermingles with apparently opposed images of organicity. In addition to being "that terrible spit-fire machine" (44), it also becomes "his machine stiffly risen at me," and "a column of the whitest ivory" (46). The penises of *Memoirs* in general combine organic and mechanical images, but Cleland's representations of Charles's penis are central to the idyllic exemplarity of this particular episode. In positioning the penis between the unmotivated organicity of nature and the artifice of the mechanism, Cleland greatly enriches his store of euphemisms.[23] More importantly, he uses both uses organic and mechanical metaphors strategically to reinforce the penis as a locus of unmotivated male sexuality. The roots and branches of Charles's male organ differ from its machinelike qualities in the same way that unintended nature differs from the artifice of the mechanical, but neither organic penises nor penis-machines can themselves *intend* to be sexual or can *will* desire for an appropriate sexual object into being; both the organic and the mechanical aspects of Charles's sexuality refer to the same unconscious and *unintendable* upwelling of sexual desire characteristic of real men.[24] Fanny may aestheticize Charles's penis in a way that undercuts the naturalness and immediacy of the sexual difference she means to assert, but her strategy for an aesthetics of the penis at least remains unified.

Cleland's rhetoric of heterosexual complementarity implies, as we have seen above, a necessary difference between male and female sexual organs. Fanny's sexuality seems to reside most self-evidently in the penetrable "quick" of her "seat of pleasure." Charles's sexual organ typically penetrates Fanny in the place "most dedicated to its reception," so that male and female bodies correspond through difference to form a synergistic whole. There are, though, moments when this synergistic wholeness gives way either to an incompatibility between "corresponding" male and female parts, or to a kind of parodic similarity that qualifies Cleland's assertions about any natural sexual correspondence.

Why, for instance, if male and female parts are "dedicated" to each other, is the moment of penetration such a violent scene? When

Fanny seduces Will, Mr. H's manservant, she recalls his insertion as a storm of physical aggression that she eagerly welcomes:

> But he did not long abuse my patience, for the objects before him had now put him by all his, and coming out with that formidable machine of his, he lets the fury loose, and pointing it directly to the pouting-lipt mouth, that bid him sweet defiance in dumb-shew, squeezes in the head, and driving with refreshed' rage, breaks in, and plugs up the whole passage of that soft-pleasure-conduit, where he makes all shake again, and put once more all within me into such an uproar, as nothing could still, but a fresh inundation from the very engine of those flames, as well as from all the springs with which nature floats that recevoir of joy, when risen to its flood-mark. (77)

This episode leaves Fanny "so bruised, so batter'd, so spent with this overmatch" that she can "hardly stir." In fact, her first affair with Will leaves Fanny fearful for her ability ever to have sex again:

> The next morning, waking pretty early after a night's perfect rest and composure, it was not without some dread and uneasiness, that I thought of what innovation that tender soft system of mine might have sustain'd from the shock of a machine so siz'd for its destruction. (79)

Fanny discovers, though, that having once taken Will and survived the experience, she is now "palpably mistress of any size of man," but her fear of "the shock" of sexual intercourse, even though it turns out to be unfounded, indicates a problematic nonrelationship between natural male and female bodies and the act of intercourse, since there is a noticeable contradiction in the idea of complementary parts "so siz'd" for each other that they can effect their own destruction. Later, Will remounts Fanny in another "overmatch" of parts:

> He hesitated a little; then, settled in the passage, he makes his way up the streights of it, with a difficulty nothing more than pleasing, widening as he went, so as to distend and smooth each soft furrow: our pleasure increasing deliciously, in proportion as our mutual touch increas'd, in that so vital part of me, in which I had now taken him, all indriven, and compleatly sheath'd, and which cram'd as it was, stretch'd spliting ripe, gave it so gratefully strait an accommodation! so strict a fold! a suction so fierce, that gave and took unutterable delight! (82)

Pleasure and violence reinforce each other in Fanny's intercourse with Will without necessarily becoming the same quality. The difference between this scene and the first is that Fanny now just as violently discommodes Will's body with "so gratefully strait an accommodation" as Will practices on her by "distending and smoothing" "each soft furrow" of her "pleasure-thirsty channel" (82). Will is, at least to some extent, reshaped in Fanny's image by the narrowness of her "passage" just as she is "stretch'd" by the size of his organ; the violent reshaping that male and female organs must practice on each other is, in other words, just as effective a sign of the disproportion or nonrelation between male and female bodies as it is a symbol of their complementarity. Indeed, true pleasure in *Memoirs* is always the product of this sort of disproportion, so that if to "complement" is to "complete" or "to fill up," the line between an orifice being stuffed "as full as it could hold" or "deliciously ingorg'd" (82) and "things being push'd to odious extremities" (158) is an extremely fine one.

Such symbolic complementarity also gives way to another form of noncomplementarity between male and female when Fanny

experiences a parodic ejaculation of her own after Will first withdraws from her:

> When our mutual trance was a little over, and the young
> fellow had withdrawn that delicious stretcher, with which
> he had most plentifully drown'd all thoughts of revenge
> [against Mr. H], in the sense of actual pleasure, the widen'd
> wounded passage refunded a stream of pearly liquids, which
> flow'd down my thighs, mix'd with streaks of blood the
> marks of the ravage of that monstrous machine of his, which
> had now triumph'd over a kind of second maiden-head. . . .
> (76)

Fanny's "wounded passage" acts as an inverted or negative phallus
"refunding" semen and blood in its own right and thus displacing
the ejaculatory activity that marks Will's presence with an action
of its own. Male and female organs that are naturally complementary constitute a performative continuum in which their interactive
"fire" welds them into a greater, synergistic whole, but Fanny's
"wounded passage," far from reinforcing the difference between
male and female, actually appropriates that difference to become
more a parodic double of Will's penis than its complement.[25]

Another powerful example of the fallibility of referential sexual
difference, and one that firmly locates the mechanisms of that difference in the world of human intentionality, occurs in *Memoirs of
a Coxcomb*. Here, Delamore wishes to make love to the beautiful
young ward of lecherous Lady Oldborough. Since Lady Oldborough
herself has sexual designs on Delamore's body, she decides to stage
a scenario in which Agnes, the young ward, apparently betrays
Delamore's attentions by sleeping with a country lad. Ushered into
Agnes's chamber by Lady Oldborough and her servant, Mrs.
Burward, Delamore interprets the scene before him according to
Lady Oldborough's direction:

Lady Oldborough, made me observe, for I was almost blind with the fury of my passions, the hat and cloaths of a man, lying in disorder upon the chairs near the bed. They served to confirm Mrs. Burward's information about the person, as they seemed those of a plain country farmer: at this I snatched pretty abruptly the light out of the woman's hands, and leaving lady Oldborough to sustain herself as well as she could, hurried towards the bed, and drew the curtain. Agnes, the beautiful Agnes, whom I had thought so innocent, lay, under the bed-cloaths, which covered every thing but her face, and hands, buried in the profoundest sleep, which even added to her charms, new graces of tenderness and delicacy: no! never appeared she to my eyes more lovely, and more despicable. For behold! on the side of her, a young fellow, with his hand passed under her neck, and clasping her as it were to him, lay snoaring, with his eyes fast enough shut, to defy the effect of the light glaring in them; which I naturally attributed to the fatigues of his chamber-confinement of the preceding day. (227–28)

Delamore bases his opinion of Agnes on his intuitive and natural response to the situation before him, even though the passage itself is fraught with qualifications of the scene it represents: Delamore is "almost blind with the fury of his passions" but he still reads the scene competently enough to assign male and female characteristics as Lady Oldborough intends them to be read; Agnes's companion only clasps her "as it were" to "him," but that is enough for Delamore to extrapolate both the heterosexual attraction natural to men and women and its consummation, to which Delamore naturally attributes the "fatigues" of the sleeping figures. Clothes and rumors thus mark sexual difference for Delamore in a way the bodies before him cannot, so that the "hat and cloaths of a man" identify Agnes's bed companion at least as adequately as "his" hypothetical penis could, and sexual difference becomes a state conferring rather than confirming the genital identity of Delamore's rival. Eventually, Delamore learns about Lady Oldborough's plot:

> The truth, in short, was, that the whole of my discovery of Agnes and her pretended gallant, was a device, and that a coarse one enough employed on any but a novice, and framed and executed by lady Oldborough, and her worthy confidante. The person in bed with Agnes was a lusty country-girl, picked out, and disguised for the purpose, and equally innocent with her of the hellish designs upon us; as they were both thrown into that deep sleep, which had deceived me, by the common operation of drugs, given them for that effect, it is easy to imagine how the rest came to be artfully disposed, as the hat and cloaths, and hour of the night. (232)

Delamore neutralizes any possibility of lesbian sexual contact, since the issue at stake is not that women are sexual beings capable of interest in each other, but that they are not men. Delamore's explanation reinstalls the heterosexual paradigm for which sexual intercourse is a function of sexual difference and the genital reference that difference supposes, so that what Agnes and her "lusty country-girl" companion might do with each other in bed before or after "the common operation of drugs" intervenes is fundamentally less important than that female-female contact of whatever nature cannot compromise Delamore in the same way that heterosexual contact can. In this case, sexual difference is all-important to Delamore's reading of the scandalous scene, even when no such difference exists, and the most "hellish designs" turn out not to be those involving female homosexuality, but those effectively counterfeiting male heterosexuality.

Delamore's protective misreading of male heterosexuality helps to explain those scenes of perverse and displaced sexual desire which culminate in the famous moment of male sodomy near the end of *Memoirs of a Woman of Pleasure*. Among these, perhaps the most significant in terms of reading sexual difference is one in which Fanny indulges the bizarre "taste" of "a new gallant of a very singular turn":

> This was a grave, staid, solemn, elderly gentleman, whose peculiar humour was a delight in combing fine tresses of hair, and as I was perfectly headed to his taste, he us'd to come constantly at my toilette hours, when I let down my hair as loose as nature; and abandon'd it to him, to do what he pleas'd with it; and accordingly he would keep me an hour, or more, in play with it, drawing the comb through it, winding the curls round his fingers, even kissing it as he smooth'd it, and all this led to no other use of my person, or any other liberties whatever, any more than if a distinction of sexes had not existed. (153)

Fanny also remarks on this gentleman's habit of buying her kid gloves and

> then biting off their fingers ends; all of which fooleries of a sickly appetite, the old gentleman paid more liberally for, than most others did for more essential favours. This lasted till a violent cough seizing and laying him up, deliver'd me from this most innocent, and most insipid trifler; for I never heard more of him, after his first retreat. (153)

By failing to use her "person" for "more essential favours," Fanny's most insipid male trifler jeopardizes the "distinction of sexes" separating him from her without necessarily jeopardizing the erotic status of his encounters. The gentleman is something of an anomaly in Fanny's sexual catalogue: a gallant uninterested in the purposive resolution of heterosexual associations hardly qualifies as a "gallant" in Fanny's system and may not even qualify as a man.[26] Since, though, Fanny records his presence and interests in her sexual confessions, his adventures indicate how the eroticism of sexual contact need not necessarily coincide perfectly with heterosexual copulation or with sexually distinct bodies to satisfy sexual desire, and even if Fanny herself experiences no desire for her partner or the activities in which he is involved, she still interprets the scene as one where sexual gratification is possible.[27]

Moreover, this scene, which appears at first reading to question the old man's masculinity in relation to the novel's normative heterosexual code of performative complementarity, actually works to recuperate the heterosexual potential of Fanny's perverse old man for the system his desires seem to overturn. It is precisely because the old man has what Fanny recognizes as "peculiar humours" in the first place that his activities are acceptable: he is both old and sick in ways that highlight his incapacity and thus make the "peculiarity" of his tastes and the insipidity of his desires nonthreatening because ultimately nonpurposive in themselves. We, as Fanny's readers, know because of her account that the old man *is* a man in his desire for Fanny's body; his misplaced attentions to her head and gloved fingers—while unsatisfactory in their own right—register, more than an appropriate sexual desire, his obvious inability to *have* an appropriate sexual desire. His "humours" are, after all, only "fooleries of a sickly appetite," but the man's very age and illness serve Fanny as a guarantee that he would have "normal" desires if only such desire were possible. The old man's interest in Fanny's body thus displaces other, more truly male acts while at the same time symbolizing those absent actions, so that the old man's fetishes represent an absent and primary heterosexuality to which both Fanny and her reader can competently refer. These legible oppositions between youth/age and health/sickness at work in

Fanny's recollection of perverse male sexuality help to prop up that sexual difference between Fanny and her elderly lover which, if left to itself, could not remain a purposive distinction between "male" and "female."

Referential sexual difference in *Memoirs* thus appears to receive its hierarchical privilege not so much from any essential appropriateness or efficacy to which it may lay claim, but rather from the way it perpetually gets read back into the erotic locus of sexual pleasure as sexuality. When, for instance, Fanny relates her brush with the two young sodomites who so nearly rear-end Cleland's novel, her account conflates narration and revision in an attempt to make the episode mean something in terms Fanny can understand. Fanny encounters the two sodomites just after Emily returns from her perverse tryst with the "handsome domino," and Fanny can read "the visible remains of the fear and confusion she had been in, still stamp'd on her countenance" (156). Fanny hears Emily's story and admits that

> I could not conceive how it was possible for mankind to run into a taste, not only universally odious, but absurd, and impossible to gratify, since, according to the notions and experience I had of things, it was not in nature to force such immense disproportions: Mrs. *Cole* only smil'd at my ignorance, and said nothing towards my undeception, which was not effected but by occular demonstration, some months after, which a most singular accident furnish'd me, and I will here set down, that I may not return again to so disagreeable a subject. (156)

Fanny's disclaimer about the impossibility of forcing nature to "such immense disproportions" seems rather disingenuous in the light of her past exploits, but it is consistent with the passage's version of the meaning of male homosexuality.[28]

When she finally encounters the two sodomites, what Fanny sees becomes indistinguishable from what she thinks she sees. What she actually witnesses is the truth, but the way she sees that truth turns it, at least initially, into the natural:

> The eldest might be, on my nearest guess, towards nineteen, a tall comely young man, in a white fustian frock, with a green velvet cape, and a cut bob-wig.
> The youngest could not be above seventeen, fair, ruddy, compleatly well made, and to say the truth, a sweet pretty stripling: He was, I fancy too, a country lad, by his dress, which was a green plush frock, and breeches of the same, white waistcoat and stockings, a jockey cap, with his yellowish hair long, and loose, in natural curls. (157)

What Fanny thinks are two men actually turn out to be just that, but only after a detour into the rhetoric of natural heterosexuality that thereafter contaminates Fanny's understanding of the episode:

> For now the elder began to embrace, to press, to kiss the younger, to put his hands in his bosom, and give such manifest signs of an amorous intention, as made me conclude the other to be a girl in disguise, a mistake that nature kept me in countenance in, for she had certainly made one, when she gave him the male stamp. (157)

The one piece of evidence this "occular demonstration" cannot give Fanny is the correct meaning of the youngster's "male stamp," even after the boy's companion uncovers the boy's "white shaft, middle-siz'd, and scarce fledg'd" (158). Faced with the epistemological gap between her knowledge and the experience before her eyes, Fanny recuperates the situation by recasting it in familiar terms. She watches as the older partner produces an engine, that certainly deserv'd to be put to a better use, and very fit to confirm me in my disbelief of the possibility of things being push'd to odious extremities, which I had built on the disproportion of parts. . . . (158)

and then recounts a scene of penetration and intercourse remarkable for its mastery of detail:

> Slipping then aside the young lad's shirt, and tucking it up under his cloaths behind, he shew'd to the open air, those globular, fleshy eminences that compose the mount-pleasants of *Rome*, and which now, with all the narrow vale that intersects them, stood display'd, and exposed to his attack: nor could I, without a shudder, behold the dispositions he made for it. First then, moistening well with spittle his instrument, obviously to render it glib, he pointed, he introduc'd it, as I could plainly discern, not only from its direction, and my losing sight of it; but by the writhing, twisting, and oft murmur'd complaints of the young sufferer; but, at length, the first streights of entrance being pretty well got through, every thing seem'd to move, and go pretty currently on, as in a carpet-road, without much rub, or resistance: and now passing one hand round his minion's hips, he got hold of his red-topt ivory toy, that stood perfectly stiff, and shewed, that if he was like his mother behind, he was like his father before. . . . (158)

Fanny authoritatively records this scene as if she knew what was going on. When the older boy moistens his "instrument" with spittle, she knows that it is "obviously to render it glib"; she "plainly discerns" the moment of penetration as such because she "loses sight" of the penetrator's shaft; she can even tell when the older partner, "renewing his driving, and thus continuing to harrass his rear," climaxes, because she understands when "the height of the fit came on with its usual symptoms, and dissmiss'd the action" (159). Fanny's description, though, consistently homogenizes the difference of this scene of homosexual intercourse as heterosexual difference even as it registers moral outrage at homosexual perversity. Fanny, for example, insists on conserving the relation between genital reference and natural sexual identity by describing the younger boy as a hermaphrodite, who "if he was like his mother behind" is still "like his father before." In a strange inversion of terms, Cleland gives us the boy's "red-topt ivory toy" as a sign to "shew" both the "mother behind" and the inappropriateness of that correspondence between male and female sites. Even more strangely, this heterosexual recuperation of perverse sexual difference turns homosexual intercourse itself into just another instance of the norm, since "the height of the fit" comes on "with its usual symptoms." Cleland reinforces this image of perverse normality by describing sodomitical activity as an instance where "every thing seem'd to move, and go pretty currently on, *as in a carpet-road.*" Sabor includes this phrase in his explanatory notes to *Memoirs* and uses an OED gloss that defines a carpet-road as "smooth, sheltered water 'near the shore, where vessels may lie at anchor in safety'" (201). If homosexual anal intercourse may meaningfully be figured as being like a carpet-road, then both its naturalness and its appropriateness must be reevaluated. If, on the one hand, the anus, like the channel of Cleland's carpet-road, is naturally a refuge for whatever "vessels" anchor safely in it, then Cleland has carefully incorporated an image of natural sexuality at the heart of his most perverse scene. If, on the other hand, anus and carpet-road must be opened out from the natural landscape, even dredged or deepened artificially, they still represent the proper sites for those activities they are intended to situate. Either way, this dramatic enactment of male sodomy rigorously reconfigures the ideology of natural heterosexuality against which its perversity is supposed to appear, since Fanny's rhetoric of heterosexual containment becomes the vehicle through which male sodomy attains a form that is readable, normal, perhaps even natural.

To shore up the difference between natural and perverse, Cleland turns to Mrs. Cole, the brothel-keeper, who has no trouble maintaining a distinction between Fanny's handsome sodomites and authentic Englishmen. Mrs. Cole declares

> *that* whatever effect this infamous passion had in other ages, and other countries, it seem'd a peculiar blessing on our air and climate, that there was a plague-spot visibly imprinted on all that are tainted with it, in this nation at least; for that among numbers of that stamp whom she had known, or at least were universally under the scandalous suspicion of it, she could not name an exception hardly of one of them, whose character was not in all other respects the most worthless and despicable that could be, stript of all the manly virtues of their own sex, and fill'd up with only the very worst vices and follies of ours. . . . (159–60)

Homosexuality bears a visible "plague-spot" announcing its presence as (1) a sign of sexual contagion or "taint," (2) a sign of national difference, and (3) a stamp-like mark supplementing the likewise visible "male stamp" (cf. 157) of apparently masculine bodies. Mrs. Cole reinforces the natural sexual difference between men and women with a further difference between those who respect natural law and "these miscreants" who "take something more precious than bread" out of the mouth of woman-kind (159). Homosexuality's visible sign marks the bearers of that "infamous passion" (159) as monstrous, or even worse:

> [I]n fine, they were scarce less execrable than ridiculous in their monstrous inconsistency, of loathing and contemning

women, and all at the same time, apeing their manners, airs, lisps, skuttle, and, in general, all their little modes of affectation, which become them at least better, than they do these unsex'd male-misses. (160)

The worst thing Mrs. Cole can think to say about homosexual men is that they imitate women's manners and affectations in a way that reveals the imitation as such. Homosexuality visibly transgresses against sexual difference by intentionally acting out that difference as a kind of parodic culture that "contemns women" while still "apeing" those "manners, airs, lisps" and so on, that "become them at least better" than such airs do men. Sexual difference as genital reference can no longer do its work as a guarantee of natural sexuality, so it must be reinscribed as a static form of cultural difference that men can intentionally assume, if not as "becomingly" as women, then at least as consciously.

This sort of intentionality underwrites the perversity of Clelandian homosexuality, as the young sodomite of Fanny's encounter makes clear when, from Fanny's perspective, he "knowingly" assumes his office as a "Ganymede" (158). To preserve this reinscription of sexual difference as an intentional cultural difference, though, that conscious assumption of a culturally feminine manner has to become a visible plague spot on the male body for both Fanny and Mrs. Cole. Otherwise, Fanny's handsome homosexuals might be mistakable for, say, a man like Charles, whose "all-perfect manly beauty" is reflected in "a face without a fault, glowing with the opening bloom, and vernal freshness of an age, in which beauty is of either sex" (44). Both Charles and the sodomites are beautiful, but Charles's physical faultlessness stands, or tries to stand, visibly in contrast to the sodomites' odious and intentional obviousness. The impossible project is, consequently, to read this cultural difference as if it were a function of genital reference and thus a part of the homosexual's legible physiology, so that the homosexual man of Fanny's and Mrs. Cole's fantasy accomplishes the incredible task of intending to be what he already is.[29]

Reading *Memoirs of a Woman of Pleasure* for the permutations of sexual difference and genital reference gives us an unstable rhetoric of bodily complementarity between male and female sites. Cleland uses this rhetoric to shore up his ideological preoccupation with natural sexuality, which must in its turn be shored up by an internal series of oppositions between youth and age, indigenous and foreign, beauty and ugliness, consciousness and body, artifice and spontaneity, all of which culminate in the broad distinction Cleland draws between Fanny's "natural" heterosexuality and the perversely conscious and therefore "cultural" activities of lesbians and homosexuals. In effect, Fanny's sodomites counterfeit masculinity as effectively as Lady Oldborough's lusty country lass does, only the sodomites use male bodies to enact their "project of preposterous pleasure" (157) and intend the acts they are caught representing. Cleland therefore affirms the mandatory superiority of heterosexuality by denigrating more cultural or assumed gender identities, but heterosexual superiority is so riven with ambiguous constructions of the body and of appropriate sexual activity that even this "moral affirmation" can be taken as a strategic stance in the contest between sexualities.[30] Cleland's proposition that the genitals locate and concentrate an innate sexual identity soon becomes the proposition that those genitals locate an appropriate sexual identity, which is itself a slight but perceptible shift from the discourse of nature to that of culture. After all, even male and female bodies engaged in recognizably sexual activities can still do inappropriate things to each other, but as long as some sign of sexual difference is discernible, Cleland's novel preserves the fiction that natural spontaneity will look like something other than the conscious agency of perversion.

Coda

This book has from its inception depended on two central assumptions. The first is that the rhetoric of heterosexual difference in eighteenth-century British literature is coherent enough as an ideological construction for its history and characteristics to be open to literary-critical analysis. My second assumption is that criticism and the politics of liberation can intersect in ways which do justice both to the historical specificity of the text and to the text's contemporary audience. I can hardly claim that this study exhausts the interpretive potential of its subjects, nor can I claim that I have mastered and exposed the rhetorical complexities of each work involved. What I can argue, and that with a fair degree of certainty, is that I place each of these works in an innovative critical context, and that as a result, these works cooperate to produce a new critical and political coherence. Each of the texts I study, from *Onania* to Cleland's *Memoirs of a Woman of Pleasure*, serves to reinforce the sociocultural authority of heterosexuality, in large part by constraining rhetorically the formal and ideological potential of the sexed body in eighteenth-century culture. If as is increasingly the case during the first half of the 1700s, the differently sexed body becomes an ineluctable norm by which all bodies, codes of conduct, and communal associations are judged, it is because of the naturalizing force of the discourse these texts exemplify.

Yet, as my reading has attempted to demonstrate, the rhetoric of sexual difference does not—because it cannot—transform the historically contingent character of heterosexuality into the seamless and transparent discourse of nature. As a consequence, the works I have examined often enact their own form of cultural critique by failing to support the logical necessity of their own arguments. My project has from the start been an attempt to read the naturalizing and consensus-building narratives of heterosexuality which emerge during the first half of the eighteenth century for their ideological discontinuities and elisions. I have, for example, tried to show how heterosexuality posits itself as an impossible antecedent for all possible sexual activity in *Onania* when it is in fact only one possible arrangement in a wide array of potentially sexual practices and communal organizations. I have tried to show how Pope strategically exploits the tenets of empiricism in his paired moral epistles to observe male character and female characterlessness while silently grounding both male-identified character and female-identified characterlessness in identical figural practices. I have tried to show how both Swift and Cleland use images of the homosexual man to define the limits of an acceptable political community based on heterosexual principles of "natural" sexual difference; equally, I hope I have shown how necessary the figure of the homosexual is to this ideal community and how impossible his exclusion turns out to be. I have tried to illustrate how Haywood organizes both liberating and conservative political narratives around the castrated male body and how castration ultimately recoups the social order of Haywood's laboring class romance.

But what finally draws my critical attention most is the degree to which each of these authors and texts participates in a discourse of violence and violation legitimized by the need to guarantee sexual difference and the stability of the male/female binarism. Whether it is the juridical violence practiced against the hermaphroditic body in *Onania*, the political violence of Swift's sodomizing political rhetoric, the compression of women's lives and experiences in Pope's *Moral Epistles*, the castrating violation of Bellamont's beautiful body in *Philidore and Placentia*, or the violent alienation of the sodomitical body in *Memoirs of a Woman of Pleasure*, the stability of heterosexual difference depends upon our rhetorical ability to suture and to erase the discontinuities that sexuality and the body inevitably leave in their discursive path.

My readings, if they have succeeded at all, have done so because they take these eighteenth-century texts at their word and try to work the internal logics of heterosexual difference out to their conclusion while at the same time remaining sensitive to the authorial sleights of hand by which natural heterosexuality seems to have succeeded without first having carried the burden of its own ideological contradictions. I have argued, in short, that my readings remain faithful to the truth of these texts even as I regard that truth with thoroughgoing suspicion and occasional hostility. Pope was, when all is said and done, no advocate for the independent rights of women, and Swift was no advocate for the equal social standing of sodomites. Given the combination of canonical standing and historical influence these texts embody, their cumulative effect remains powerful. And as long as such works utilize fundamental principles of misogyny and homophobia to maintain the privileged stance of heterosexual difference, we must continually and thoroughly reexamine the uses to which we put those works.

Notes

Introduction: Sexuality and the "Natural" Subject of the Early Eighteenth Century

1. *Desire and Domestic Fiction* (Oxford: Oxford University Press, 1987), 24.

2. *Ends of Empire: Women and Ideology in Early Eighteenth Century English Literature* (Ithaca, N.Y.: Cornell University Press, 1993), 3.

3. *Making Sex: Body and Gender from the Greeks to Freud* (Cambridge: Harvard University Press, 1990), 149.

4. "The Birth of the Queen," in *Hidden from History: Reclaiming the Gay and Lesbian Past*, ed. Martin Duberman, Martha Vicinus, and George Chauncey Jr. (New York: New American Library, 1989), 130.

5. Ibid., 131.

6. This description of Sedley's activities comes from Samuel Pepys's diary entry for 1 July 1663, and as Cameron McFarlane notes, Pepys seems peculiarly confused by the scene he has just described in such a detailed fashion. McFarlane cites Pepys's bewildered "knowingness" as tacit recognition that "the image of a male desiring another male gains a surprising cultural prominence" during the Restoration, but that such prominence in itself does not mean that "this move toward specificity had

181

the result of making *sodomite* identical to *homosexual,* let alone *gay.*" I would ask further if Pepys's knowing confusion acts as a kind of disclaimer that rehabilitates Sedley's social status. See *The Sodomite in Fiction and Satire, 1660–1750* (New York: Columbia University Press, 1997), 4.

7. "Birth of the Queen," 131.

8. "Sodomitical Subcultures, Sodomitical Roles, and the Gender Revolution of the Eighteenth Century: The Recent Historiography," in *'Tis Nature's Fault: Unauthorized Sexuality during the Enlightenment,* ed. Robert Maccubbin (Cambridge: Cambridge University Press, 1985), 117.

9. "The Pursuit of Homosexuality in the Eighteenth Century: 'Utterly Confused Category' and/or Rich Repository?" in *'Tis Nature's Fault,* ed. Maccubbin, 132.

10. *The Love that Dared Not Speak Its Name: A Candid History of Homosexuality in Britain* (Boston: Little, Brown, 1970), 36–37.

11. "Legislating the Norm: From Sodomy to Gross Indecency," in *Displacing Homophobia: Gay Male Perspectives in Literature and Culture,* ed. Ronald R. Butters, John M. Clum, and Michael Moon (Durham, N.C.: Duke University Press, 1989), 171.

12. "Birth of the Queen," 137.

13. "Legislating the Norm," 185.

14. Hyde gives a comprehensive account of Castlehaven's trial. See *Love that Dared Not Speak Its Name,* 44–57.

15. See R. B. Burg, "Ho Hum, Another Work of the Devil: Buggery and Sodomy in Early Stuart England," in *Historical Perspectives on Homosexuality,* ed. Salvatore J. Licata and Robert P. Petersen (New York: Haworth Press, 1981), 72.

16. *Love that Dared Not Speak Its Name,* 46.

17. Ibid., 47.

18. Ibid.

19. *Sodomy Trials: Seven Documents,* ed. Randolph Trumbach (New York: Garland, 1986), 12.

20. *The Crisis of the Aristocracy, 1558–1641* (Oxford: Clarendon Press, 1965), 668.

21. "Another Work of the Devil," 74.

22. *Sodomy Trials,* 25.

23. I have assigned page numbers to the unnumbered preface.

24. "Sodomitical Assaults, Gender Role, and Sexual Development in Eighteenth-Century London," in *The Pursuit of Sodomy: Male Homosexuality in Renaissance and Enlightenment Europe*, ed. Kent Gerard and Gert Hekma (New York: Harrington Park Press, 1989), 422.

25. Ibid., 422.

26. "Birth of the Queen," 130.

27. *Making Sex*, 149–50.

28. See Peter Wagner's "The Veil of Medicine and Morality: Some Pornographic Aspects of the *Onania*," *British Journal for Eighteenth-Century Studies* 2 (1983): 179, for this publication date.

Chapter 1. Onania: *Self-Pollution and the Danger of Female Sexuality*

Portions of this chapter were first presented as part of the "New Gay Science" panel during the NEASECS conference at Yale University in October 1993.

1. By the time we reach Crouch's 1723 edition, *Onania* falls into four major divisions: the first chapter concerning "the heinous sin of self-pollution"; the second chapter concerning "the frightful consequences of self-pollution"; the third chapter concerning "spiritual and physical advice to those who have injur'd themselves by the abominable practice of self-pollution"; and the *Supplement*, which records much of the anti-Onanist's putative correspondence and from which most of the material for this chapter is drawn.

2. *Onania; or the Heinous Sin of Self-Pollution*, 8th ed. (1723; reprint, vol. 12 of the Garland series, *Marriage, Sex and the Family in England, 1660-1800*, New York: Garland, 1986), title page. I have chosen to use this edition because it is the only readily available facsimile of *Onania*. Subsequent page references will be cited in the body of the text.

3. The original publication date for *Onania* remains uncertain. Wagner's "The Veil of Medicine and Morality," 179, puts the date circa 1708, as opposed to Stone. The *Supplement* seems to have been published still later, as it would have to have been if the anti-Onanist's claims about the veracity of its letters are to be believed.

4. *The Family, Sex, and Marriage in England, 1500–1800* (New York: Harper and Row, 1979), 320.

5. *Disease and Representation: Images of Illness from Madness to AIDS* (Ithaca, N.Y.: Cornell University Press, 1988), 69–70.

6. "Authority and Masturbation: Some Remarks on a Bibliographical Investigation," *Yearbook of Psychoanalysis* 9(1953): 116.

7. Ibid.

8. *Dr. [Richard?] Carr's Medicinal Epistles upon Several Occasions*, trans. John Quincy (London: printed for William Newton, near the Pump in Little-Britain, and J. Phillips in Cornhill, 1714). Copy in Mann Library, Cornell University. This letter is included in its entirety in the *Supplement to the Onania*, 155–62.

9. *Representations* 14 (1986): 2.

10. Julia Epstein analyzes the case of a possible eighteenth-century French hermaphrodite named Anne Grandjean and writes that Grandjean was attacked in the nineteenth century because he/she "'se faisait passer publiquement pour homme et femme à la fois' (. . . passed himself off [in public] as a man and as a woman simultaneously) and [was] "une femme, dont les parties offraient un prolongement anormal, comme autrefois les femmes de Lesbos' (a woman whose organs were abnormally elongated, as was the case in antiquity with the women of Lesbos); it is not clear what it would mean to be a man and at the same time a woman, and the analogy to the women of Lesbos elucidates this writer's assumption of homosexuality as well as his ignorance of the Grandjean case" ("Either/ Or—Neither/Both: Sexual Ambiguity and the Ideology of Gender," *Genders* 7 [1990]: 118). Grandjean's disposition towards anatomical indeterminacy, and especially his/her "elongated organs," clearly exemplifies the relation between clitoral enlargement and hermaphroditic, masculinized homosexuality. Elsewhere, Epstein comments on a reference to Dr. Carr's two Roman nuns and writes, "Hermaphrodites highlight the privilege differential between male and female precisely because they cannot participate neatly in it. In addition, their illicit 'usurpation' of a gender not theirs by birth registration always raises the specter of homosexuality" (124).

11. Dr. Carr closes his letter with the story of another monstrously proximate oddity, a sexually mature infant, and observes that "NATURE, refuses to be circumscribed in her Operations, but yet she has never been

known to make such Excursions as this must have been; we ought therefore to stand in wonder at her exact Regularities, because of our Inability in following her through all her Works" (*Supplement*, 161). By thus emphasizing natural predictability in the face of the anomalous, Carr recoups such instances of "uncommon" sexuality as expressions of natural regularity operating at some level deeper than their anomalous surface.

12. In terms of a heterosexual teleology.

13. Randolph Trumbach argues that the early eighteenth century sees a shift from three sexes (male, female, hermaphroditic) and two genders (male, female) to two sexes (male, female) and three genders (male, female, effeminate sodomite). As a transitional text from one system to another, *Onania*'s sexual epistemology can be seen as depending on the physical mutability of the older system while at the same time requiring the stable "female" gender of the developing ideology. See "London's Sapphists: From Three Sexes to Four Genders in the Making of Modern Culture," in *Bodyguards: The Cultural Politics of Gender Ambiguity*, ed. Julia Epstein and Kristina Straub (New York: Routledge, 1991), esp. 112–15.

14. The imperative to choose one sexual identity absolutely conflates "gender" and "sex" as the sexual and reproduces the binarism male/female in the place of the hermaphrodite's disturbing performative potential. To become a lawful subject, in other words, the hermaphrodite must pass from a multiple to a univocal state so as to produce "sex" as constative and "the law" as performative.

15. "An Hermophrodite [*sic*], is by all look'd upon as a Creature of vile Deformity, bringing a Shame upon both Sexes; and in old Times, wherever found, were drowned or made away with, such Monsters not being thought by them fit to live" (*Supplement*, 165).

16. Jill Campbell has argued in her "'When Men Women Turn': Gender Reversals in Fielding's Plays" that Fielding's fascination with, and fear of, the castrato and of the male impersonator register a sense of the phallus's inability ever completely and reliably to guarantee the gender distinction giving the two sexes their meaning: "When the phallus, counted on to insure so much, becomes indistinguishable from an inanimate impersonation of life . . . then the castrato appears too typical, and the male impersonator emerges as too powerful, too capable of convincingly wearing the breeches which the man, after all, only filled with something not really his

own" (*The New Eighteenth Century* [New York: Methuen, 1987], 82). Since the hermaphrodite and, by the anti-Onanist's own extension, the masturbating woman embody the theatrical appropriation Fielding fears, this notion of "transferability" operates, I think, in a similar fashion in *Onania*.

17. Epstein theorizes that "when efforts at taxonomy yield ambiguity, they fail; ambiguity must be officially erased in order to defeat the threat of rule breaking, boundary crossing, and anarchy that occurs if gender-indeterminate individuals are permitted to marry at their discretion, to form legal bonds in which the sexes of the partners may be the same or ambiguous and therefore potentially the same. The threat here comes from all sides; if we digress from the absoluteness of the binary gender opposition, we will have a state in which bourgeois hegemony is threatened because homosexuality may claim sanctions, and social and legal control over the body —both social and anatomic—will thereby be threatened" ("Either/Or," 129).

Chapter 2. Swift and the Political Anus

1. Wood was the British ironmonger and coiner who in 1722 convinced Robert Walpole's government to grant him a patent for producing copper halfpence for the Irish economy. Swift was concerned that "Wood's halfpence" would swamp Ireland, supplant legal gold and silver tender, and ruin Ireland's already meager economic prospects. For further details, see Irvin Ehrenpreis, *Dean Swift*, vol. 3 of *Swift: The Man, His Works, and the Age* (Cambridge: Harvard University Press, 1983), 187–97.

2. "A Serious Poem Upon William Wood," in *Jonathan Swift: The Complete Poems*, ed. Pat Rogers (New Haven: Yale University Press, 1983).

3. Ehrenpreis prefaces his discussion of the Drapier's career by arguing that, while Swift was not first to lead the cause against Wood's patent, his intervention proved decisive both for himself and for Ireland: "But in the most triumphant accomplishment of his whole career, Swift began as a follower. The initiative and the programme belonged to others; and if Swift did come to serve as champion, it was because those in the van invited him to join them. Yet without Swift the cause would have remained narrow and insular. He raised it from the bleakness of one more chapter

of British mistreatment of Ireland to be an illustration of our concept of liberty. Still, the first materials for his brilliant design were supplied to him by simpler minds" (*Dean Swift*, 187). Whether or not the Drapier incident was as climactic to either Swift or Ireland as Ehrenpreis claims is less important than that the incident has traditionally been seen in Swift criticism as the high point of Swift's political activity.

4. Donald Greene, for example, interprets "The Lady's Dressing Room," "Cassinus and Peter," and "Strephon and Chloe" as using shit to espouse a sober Christian heterosexual ethic. Greene criticizes Norman O. Brown for believing that the contradiction in "Cassinus and Peter" between being in love and knowing the beloved shits is really Swift's. See "On Swift's 'Scatological' Poems," in *Essential Articles for the Study of Jonathan Swift's Poetry*, ed. David M. Vieth (Hamden, Conn.: Shoe String Press, 1984), 232.

5. *Life Against Death: The Psychoanalytic Meaning of History* (Middletown, Conn.: Wesleyan University Press, 1985), 179.

6. Much of Jae Num Lee's *Swift and Scatological Satire* (Albuquerque: University of New Mexico Press, 1971) is devoted to the excremental anality of Swift's poetry and is largely a reaction to Brown's interpretive methods. See pages 1–2 and 92–93. Carol Houlihan Flynn writes that "Swift's vision of unconfined man freely offering that deepest, most anal part of himself inspired Norman O. Brown to celebrate Swift for his radical anticipation of Freud in his awareness of the centrality of anal eroticism" (*The Body in Swift and Defoe* [Cambridge: Cambridge University Press, 1990], 95). Awareness of man's "deepest, most anal part of himself" is thus for Flynn somehow an implicit acknowledgment that profound anality is always excremental.

7. Eve Sedgwick acknowledges both the slippage between cultural ideas of "gender" and biological implications of "sexuality" as theoretical terms and the political efficacy of considering these terms as separable. Briefly, if "sexuality" coordinates, however problematically, with the biological register, "gender, then is the far more elaborated, more fully and rigidly dichotomized social production and reproduction of male and female identities and behaviors—of male and female *persons*—in a cultural system for which "male/female" functions as a primary and perhaps model binarism affecting the structure and meaning of many, many other

binarisms whose apparent connection to chromosomal sex will often be exiguous or nonexistent" (*Epistemology of the Closet* [Berkeley: University of California Press, 1990]), 27–28. I attempt to separate the two terms in my reading of Swift's poetry so that the radically different "sexual" fates of similarly sexed bodies will be apparent. Masculinity as *gender* often plays a deciding role in the *sexual* relation one man has with others in Swift's poems. This terminological difference will consequently be of particular importance to my reading of same-sex rape scenes.

8. Quoted in Cohen, "Legislating the Norm," 176.

9. Quoted in Hyde, *Love that Dared Not Speak Its Name*, 37.

10. See Rousseau, "Pursuit of Homosexuality in the Eighteenth Century," 132–33, 136–37.

11. See Trumbach, "Sodomitical Subcultures," 112, for a discussion of the symbolic proscription of the anus in Christian society and the possibility that an anally identified scapegoat provided convenient relief in times of civil stress.

12. *The Writings of Jonathan Swift*, ed. Robert A. Greenberg and William Bowman Piper (New York: Norton, 1973), 221.

13. Deborah Baker Wyrick provides an intelligent reading of Swift's punning technique in her analysis of "A Serious Poem," but her account fails to factor in Swift's images of sodomy even when dealing with Wood as "a new groaning board." See *Jonathan Swift and the Vested Word* (Chapel Hill: University of North Carolina Press, 1988), 164.

14. *Energy and Order in the Poetry of Swift* (Lewisburg, Pa.: Bucknell University Press, 1980), 71–72.

15. "Birth of the Queen," 130–31, my emphasis.

16. The last execution for sodomy in England took place in 1836. See "Legislating the Norm," 190.

17. Tighe seems originally to have offended Swift by informing Lord Carteret about a politically indiscreet sermon by Thomas Sheridan, Swift's protégé. Sheridan preached on the text, "Sufficient to the day is the evil thereof," on the anniversary of the king's accession, 1 August 1725. Tighe made sure that news of Sheridan's blunder reached Carteret, the lord lieutenant of Ireland, and Sheridan lost his chance for further preferment. See Ehrenpreis, *Dean Swift*, 362–65.

18. *Jonathan Swift: The Complete Poems*, ed. Rogers, 776.

19. Ibid., 776–77.

20. The *Intelligencer* prints these ten lines not found in the Faulkner edition.

21. See Ehrenpreis, *Dean Swift*, 579–80, for the identification of Irish politics and Tighe with puppet theater.

22. *Jonathan Swift: The Complete Poems*, ed. Rogers, 895. Rogers includes the poem in Swift's works and argues that "no one has produced any good reason to disturb the contemporary evidence which allots the poem, in its earliest conception at least, to Swift alone" (896). John Butt attributes the poem to Pope and includes it among Pope's minor verse in his edition of Pope's works. See *The Poems of Alexander Pope* (New Haven: Yale University Press, 1963), 823–26.

23. *Jonathan Swift: The Complete Poems*, ed. Rogers, 898.

24. "Politics and Sexuality in Portraits of John, Lord Hervey," *Word and Image* 6 (1990): 281.

25. Ibid., 281–82.

26. *Jonathan Swift: The Complete Poems*, ed. Rogers, 779–80, for this publication date.

27. Ibid., 780.

Chapter 3. Pope's To Cobham *and* To a Lady: Empiricism and the Synecdochic Woman

1. On this pairing see Miriam Leranbaum, *Alexander Pope's "Opus Magnum,"* 1729–1744 (Oxford: Clarendon Press, 1977), especially the third chapter; see also Laura Brown, *Alexander Pope* (Oxford: Basil Blackwell, 1985), 101: "Epistle II, *To a Lady* (1735), the last published of the *Epistles to Several Persons*, has been read as a systematic parallel to the *Epistle to Cobham*."

2. See, for example, discussions of character in Benjamin Boyce, *The Theophrastan Character in England to 1642* (Cambridge: Harvard University Press, 1947); and idem, *The Character-Sketches in Pope's Poems* (Durham, N.C.: Duke University Press, 1962). For discussions of the history and meaning of the "character" in Pope's work, see, in addition to Brown, Patricia Meyer Spacks, *An Argument of Images: The Poetry of Alexander Pope* (Cambridge: Harvard University Press, 1971); David B.

Morris, *Alexander Pope: The Genius of Sense* (Cambridge: Harvard University Press, 1984); F. V. Bogel, *Acts of Knowledge: Pope's Later Poems* (Lewisburg, Pa.: Bucknell University Press, 1981); Felicity Nussbaum, "Pope's 'To a Lady' and the Eighteenth-Century Woman," *Philological Quarterly* 54 (1975): 444–56; and idem, *The Brink of All We Hate: English Satires on Women, 1660–1750* (Lexington: University Press of Kentucky, 1984), as well as Ellen Pollak, *The Poetics of Sexual Myth: Gender and Ideology in the Verse of Swift and Pope* (Chicago: University of Chicago Press, 1985).

3. Boyce argues that "one is tempted to propose the neat generalization that in Pope's depictions the type tends to become more individual and the individual more typical" (*Character-Sketches in Pope's Poems*, 75), while in response to Boyce, Spacks comments that "it is a perceptive observation on the poet's technique . . . where the emotional fluctuation, conflict, and anguish of 'the sex' are so exactly specified that they are responded to as if to the emotions of an individual" (*Argument of Images*, 165). Bogel, on the other hand, sees type and individual pulling further away from each other as the generalization comes to represent a "schematic" reduction of experience to type. Individuals in the *Epistles* can in Pope's most felicitous moments, though, embody the "substantial" knowledge of mature cognition (see *Acts*, 89–90).

4. Bogel has argued that the theory of the ruling passion that dominates the analysis of character in both *To Cobham* and *To a Lady* "is a hypothesis urging, first, that a search for some sort of unity govern the examination of character, and second, that this unity be sought at the level of the passions" (*Acts*, 84). The ruling passion reconciles appearance and reality because "the apparent chaos of [man's] thoughts and actions is supported by a substratum of consistency" (ibid., 85). David Morris traces the notions of inconsistency and inconstancy as they work in the *Epistles* and finds that while "Pope's theory of character in the *Moral Essays* seems to contain inconsistencies serious enough to reach the point of paradox or self-contradiction" (*Alexander Pope*, 196), the ideas of inconsistency and inconstancy remain stable enough to serve as trustworthy categorizing principles in themselves: "For Pope, as we have seen, all individuals are characterized by inconsistency, but such variation necessarily

implies the existence of a central, stable character against which variation may be measured. . . . Inconstancy, by contrast, involves a much more radical kind of change. It does not imply variation from or within a firm, centered, consistent character. Inconstancy suggests the absence of any center. Character becomes the focus of oppositions so extreme and changes so unceasing that there is a real question whether character still exists" (ibid., 200–201).

5. *Theophrastan Character*, 152–53.

6. Ironically, Boyce begins his discussion of character theory with an anecdote describing Elizabeth I's desire not to have the individuality of her features lost or obscured by the generic "shadowing" of court portraiture. See ibid., 152.

7. See note 2, above.

8. William Warburton, *The Works of Alexander Pope Esq. In Nine Volumes Complete. . . . Together with the Commentary and Notes of Mr. Warburton* (1751), reprinted in *Pope: The Critical Heritage*, ed. John Barnard (London: Routledge and Kegan Paul, 1973), 363.

9. Brown, *Alexander Pope*, 101.

10. Pollak, *Poetics of Sexual Myth*, 123.

11. Specifically, Thomas Edwards in *This Dark Estate: A Reading of Pope* (Berkeley: University of California Press, 1963). Edwards suggests that *To a Lady* refers to all of human existence because its satire "yields to something like a tragic view of the effects of time and change that everyone—women and men alike—must someday confront and yield to" (73). For a counterargument to this position, see Pollak, *Poetics of Sexual Myth*, 118–19.

12. Quotations from the Epistles will be from *Epistles to Several Persons*, ed. F. W. Bateson, vol. 3, bk. 2 of *The Twickenham Edition of the Poems of Alexander Pope*, general ed. John Butt (New Haven: Yale University Press, 1951). Line and page references will be cited in the body of the text.

13. Morris contends that Pope moves, in the *Epistles*, from an Aristotelian conception of character expressed as action to one in which character is the effect of an individual psychological dynamic: "Pope's most innovative contribution to English theories of character is his effort, following

Montaigne, to shift the locus of character from external actions or social roles or physiological humors to the mind. He explicitly rejects the Aristotelian doctrine that character is equivalent to action. For Pope, on the contrary, it is often impossible to understand character by studying actions—to 'Infer the Motive from the Deed'. He moves close to the Lockean position that would equate identity with consciousness, except he also insists that consciousness is often unaware of its own 'dim' sources and motives" (*Alexander Pope*, 199). We should recognize, however, that Pope gives preference to empirical observation even when discussing the limitations of its role in knowing character. In other words, I question whether the empiricism of Pope's psychology is meant more as an aid in the Lockean search for self-knowledge than as a strategic promotion of masculine prerogative.

14. Spacks describes the paired masculine binarisms that pervade *To Cobham* as part of a concretizing representational process by which the reader gains access to the poem's forms of knowledge: "Earliness and lateness, madness and wisdom, drunkenness and civility, friendliness and faithlessness—each characteristic has a socially sanctioned appropriateness to a special context which the reader can readily imagine. But these 'images' are more psychic than physical: the locus of reality is interior. They function not quite as metaphors but as emblems. In their neat contrasting pairings they sum up the orderly inconsistencies that compose a man" (*Argument of Images*, 10). Indeed, Pope's epistle on male character depends upon this paradoxical conceit of a regularized inconsistency for much of its rhetorical force.

15. Brown has observed that "the ruling passion repudiates the paradox of the first half of the epistle, and consequently the thematization of the doubtful role of the observer in judging human character fades from the poem when this claim to resolution is made" (*Alexander Pope*, 100).

16. Bogel, *Acts*, 84.

17. This explains the pressure Pope exerts on the act of "seeing," which correlates a visual referent with appropriate acts of poetic representation. As Spacks writes about a key summary of female character in *To a Lady* (lines 243–48), "the six-line summary contains no verbs, except the opening imperative 'See' (a verb that recurs frequently in this poem of images);

this syntactical omission suggests in mimetic terms the purposelessness, the lack of meaningful activity ('Fair to no purpose, artful to no end,' line 245), characteristic of these women" (*Argument of Images*, 165). See also Pollak, *Poetics of Sexual Myth*, 120. For Pope, as for Warburton, poetic "vision" is a quasi-empirical reproduction of physical observation.

18. Jonathan Culler, *Structuralist Poetics* (London: Routledge and Kegan Paul, 1975), 180–81.

19. Jonathan Culler, "The Turns of Metaphor," in *The Pursuit of Signs: Semiotics, Literature, Deconstruction* (Ithaca, N.Y.: Cornell University Press, 1981), 190.

20. In "Ideology and Ideological State Apparatuses," reprinted in *Subjectivity and Social Relations* (Philadelphia: Open University Press, 1985), 80, Louis Althusser writes, "[I]t follows that, for you and me, the category of the subject is a primary 'obviousness' (obviousnesses are always primary): it is clear that you and I are subjects (free, ethical, etc. . . .). Like all obviousnesses, including those that make a word 'name a thing' or 'have a meaning' (therefore including the obviousness of the 'transparency' of language), the 'obviousness' that you and I are subjects—and that that does not cause any problems—is an ideological effect, the elementary ideological effect. It is indeed a peculiarity of ideology that it imposes (without appearing to do so, since these are 'obviousnesses') obviousnesses as obviousnesses, which we cannot *fail to recognize* and before which we have the inevitable and natural reaction of crying out (aloud or in the 'still, small voice of conscience'): 'That's obvious! That's right! That's true!'"

21. Indeed, the first 173 lines of *To Cobham* thematize the problem of objective observation.

22. *To Cobham,* line 24.

23. Both bell hooks and Judith Butler identify the "ethnographic" tendency of such a perspective to colonize its object from a position of authorial power. See Butler's discussion of the film, *Paris is Burning,* in *Bodies that Matter* (New York: Routledge, 1993), 121–40. Butler concludes with hooks that "within this culture the ethnographic conceit of a neutral gaze will always be a white gaze, an unmarked white gaze, one which passes its own perspective off as the omniscient, one which presumes upon and enacts its own perspective as if it were no perspective at all" (136), but she

also perceptively questions whether or not the colonizer's perspective remains unconditioned by the subjectivity it records.

24. See Pollak, *Poetics of Sexual Myth*, 208 n. 9.

25. For metaphor's privileged essentializing function and the interrelationship of metonymy and metaphor, see Culler, "Turns of Metaphor." See also Culler's discussion of synecdoche and metaphor in *Structuralist Poetics*, 180–81.

26. "Turning" is an act specifically associated with Atossa that suggests the passage of time and invokes an empirically noticeable action (see *To a Lady*, line 116).

27. *Alexander Pope and the Traditions of Formal Verse Satire* (Princeton: Princeton University Press, 1982), 196.

28. These women conform to the self-annihilating pattern David Morris describes when he distinguishes between inconsistency, which he considers part of Pope's human condition, and inconstancy, which involves a radical dysfunction of opposites. See *Alexander Pope*, 200–201.

29. By "thematic" I mean that line of argument consistent with the poem's misogynist project.

30. For *epanados*, see *A Handbook to Literature*, 8th ed., by William Harmon and C. Hugh Holman (Upper Saddle River, N.J.: Prentice-Hall, 2000), 188.

31. Atossa has been identified variously as Sarah, duchess of Marlborough and Katherine Darnley, duchess of Buckinghamshire (see *Epistles to Several Persons*, 57). This uncertainty as to Atossa's true identity would seem to reinforce the claim that Pope generates his character by generalizing from the particulars of individual lives. But Wharton represents both Philip, duke of Wharton, and an abstraction based upon the man, suggesting that the difference between observed "original" and generic "abstraction" inheres in Pope's poems less as an absolute distinction than as a strategy.

32. Leranbaum assumes that Cobham's putative last words are morally superior because they are spiritual and patriotic in tone, while the crone's and Narcissa's utterances are more basely material. The effect of Leranbaum's assumption, however, is to recuperate gender-specific class distinctions for Pope. But the structure of these utterances remains the same for each character despite Pope's class-enforced misogyny.

Chapter 4. Haywood's Philidore and Placentia, or What the Eunuch Lost

1. See *Popular Fiction Before Richardson: Narrative Patterns, 1700–1739* (Oxford: Clarendon Press, 1969), 179.

2. Ibid., 181.

3. Pope included Haywood in the *Dunciad* of 1728, where she remained an object of ridicule through the 1743 edition.

4. See Mary Anne Schofield, *Eliza Haywood* (Boston: Twayne, 1985), 43.

5. *Popular Fiction*, 169–70.

6. *The Origins of the English Novel, 1600–1740* (Baltimore: Johns Hopkins University Press, 1987), 260–62.

7. *Seductive Forms: Women's Amatory Fiction from 1684 to 1740* (Oxford: Clarendon Press, 1992).

8. "'I Died for Love': Esteem in Eighteenth-Century Novels by Women," in *Fetter'd or Free? British Women Novelists, 1670–1815*, ed. Mary Anne Schofield and Cecilia Macheski (Athens: Ohio University Press, 1986), 156–57.

9. *Quiet Rebellion: The Fictional Heroines of Eliza Fowler Haywood* (Washington, D.C.: University Press of America, 1982), 28.

10. Ibid., 39.

11. Ibid.

12. Ibid., 38.

13. *Philidore and Placentia, or L'Amour trop Délicat*, reprinted in *Four before Richardson: Selected English Novels, 1720–1727*, ed. William H. McBurney (Lincoln: University of Nebraska Press, 1963), 157. Subsequent page numbers will be cited in the body of the text.

14. Congreve famously defines the *romance* in the preface to his 1692 work, *Incognita*: "Romances are generally composed of the constant loves and invincible courages of heroes, heroines, kings, and queens, mortals of the first rank where lofty language, miraculous contingencies, and impossible performances elevate and surprise the reader into giddy delight." See Lore Metzger's introduction to the Norton edition of *Oroonoko, or the Royal Slave* (New York: Norton, 1973), x.

15. Quoted in Jane Spencer, *The Rise of the Woman Novelist: From Aphra Behn to Jane Austen* (Oxford: Basil Blackwell, 1986), 182.

16. *Popular Fiction*, 175–76.

17. *Seductive Forms*, 35.

18. I consider the question of proportion at greater length in chapter 5 when I discuss Cleland's *Memoirs of a Coxcomb*. See 142–43.

19. Perhaps it would be more accurate to read this scene as occurring beyond any social context. The exotic Persian locale in which Philidore encounters the beautiful young man is, after all, a fantastic and utopian space that by definition transgresses the conventions of British society. Coming as it does after the shipwreck and the tiger attack, Philidore's meeting with Bellamont is marked throughout with the signs of an eroticized Eastern culture where English swords penetrate Persian male bodies with perfect ease (*Philidore and Placentia*, 188). The effect of such homoerotic exoticism is to release Haywood's characters, at least briefly, from those cultural identities which define and constrain them as Englishmen. If, for the moment, Philidore and Bellamont exist outside of the class and gender conventions that otherwise bind them, then Haywood's novel makes two radical suggestions: first, the scene's homoerotic potential is deliberate and not an accident of Haywood's prose; and second, by identifying with Haywood's characters, her readers may experience the transgressive pleasure of a momentary but nevertheless significant unbinding of otherwise immutable social relations.

20. *Between Feminism and Psychoanalysis* (London: Routledge, 1989), 4.

21. Schofield argues that it is Arithea's aggressiveness that costs Bellamont his manhood: "The Christian Eunuch and Arithea echo the main story of Philidore and Placentia's affair; however, they represent no positive championing of the properly ordered roles for man and woman. Theirs remains an impotent love, impossible to fulfill. When woman remains the aggressor, the affair cannot be consummated" (*Quiet Rebellion*, 41). While there is a certain validity to this interpretation, Schofield fails to recognize the degree to which Bellamont's castration calls into question the stability of such "properly ordered roles for man and woman," and she misses the kind of transgressive play that the scene of Bellamont's abuse and castration liberates.

22. Ann Barr Snitow, "Mass Market Romance: Pornography for Women is Different," in *Powers of Desire: The Politics of Sexuality*, ed. Ann Barr Snitow, Christine Stansell, and Sharon Thompson (New York: Monthly Review Press, 1983), 247.

23. *Popular Fiction*, 167.

24. Bellamont's role in *Philidore and Placentia* thus agrees with the larger role of romance that Jane Spencer has defined. Spencer writes, "This, surely was the main appeal of romance for the female reader: it offered escape from male-dominated reality through a fantasy of female power" (*Rise of the Woman Novelist*, 184).

Chapter 5. Reading the Rhetoric of Sexual Difference in Cleland's Memoirs of a Woman of Pleasure

1. "The Mythology of Love: Venerean (and related) Iconography in Pope, Fielding, Cleland, and Sterne," in *Sexuality in Eighteenth-Century Britain*, ed. Paul-Gabriel Boucé (Manchester: Manchester University Press, 1982), 184.

2. Brooks-Davies cites book 3 of Spenser's *Faerie Queene*, which moves from the homosexual relationship between Phebus and Hyacinthus to Venus's coupling with Adonis, as a precursor to the tale of heterosexual love in *Memoirs*. In doing so, he implicitly identifies male homosexuality with Fanny's immature lesbianism and subordinates both practices to mature heterosexuality: "At *Faerie Queene*, III. Vi. 45-6, we are led through homosexuality (Phoebus and Hyacinthus) and Narcissus before being allowed to encounter Venus and Adonis" (195 n. 42). Fanny thus seems strangely assimilated by a model of male sexuality; the point, though, is that *Memoirs*, like its Spenserian referent, moves in Brooke-Davies's reading from a "preliminary" same-sex association to a "final" model of heterosexual activity based on the appropriate sexual differences.

3. *Eighteenth Century: Theory and Interpretation* 22(1981): 51.

4. Julia Epstein expresses a similar point of view in "Fanny's Fanny: Epistolarity, Eroticism, and the Transsexual Text," in *Writing the Female Voice: Essays on Epistolary Literature*, ed. Elizabeth Goldsmith (Boston: Northeastern University Press, 1989). Epstein writes, "Between Fanny's

early sexual initiation and the reunion of these true lovers [Fanny and Charles], she samples a comprehensive array of human sexual experience: from voyeurism to lesbianism, from masturbation to heterosexual inter-course, from flagellation to fetishism to group orgies, Fanny's 'animal spir-its' are titillated and satisfied. Cleland's text, however does not focus, as one might suppose from its plot, on the aroused female body. It offers instead a celebration of male genitalia, of the aroused male, and of ideal-ized and invincible male sexual prowess: the phallus is everywhere and is everywhere worshipped. Woven through Fanny's sexual adventures is the always primary return to Cleland's fantasy of overpowering conventional heterosexuality" (136). Even if Epstein is right in placing the phallus at the center of the network of significations of the *Memoirs,* we should ask how the omnipresence of the phallus equals an "always primary" return to heterosexuality.

    5. "Seeing Sodomy: *Fanny Hill*'s Blinding Vision," in *Homosexual-ity in Renaissance and Enlightenment England,* ed. Claude Summers (New York: Harrington Park Press, 1992), 180.

    6. *Memoirs of a Woman of Pleasure,* ed. Peter Sabor (Oxford: Ox-ford University Press, 1985), 160. All citations are from this edition.

    7. "Some of us, unlike Fanny, get to see homosexual sodomy, if not all the time, at least often enough. But even for us, there will always have been that first sighting in which it was not so much we who discovered a new kind of sex, as a new kind of sex that saw, and showed us, who and what we had been, who and what we could no longer be. Because to envision sodomy turned out to mean our revision by sodomy. Alienated from our sense of who we were, alienated from 'sense' in its larger sense, we suddenly became the Other we were not, our own significant Other—which is to say, insignificant. At least, that is, until we discovered the other Others who we, as 'gays,' were not" ("Seeing Sodomy," 181–82). All well and good, but how many "insignificant" others can Kopelson's critical scheme accommodate?

    8. The opposition at work here is between "nature" and "culture." I agree with Nancy Armstrong, who argues that "the difference between nature and culture is always a function of culture, the construction of nature being one of culture's habitual tropes of self-authorization" (*De-sire and Domestic Fiction* [Oxford: Oxford University Press, 1987], 262).

"Naturally" sexually different bodies are, by this reading, as much an artifact as the more "cultural" gender categories supposedly derived from them.

9. Judith Butler thus provides us with a more useful theory of drag than Miller's. Butler writes, "Drag is the not putting on of a gender that belongs properly to some other group, i.e. an act of expropriation or *appro*priation that assumes that gender is the rightful property of sex, that 'masculine' belongs to 'male' and 'feminine' belongs to 'female.' There is no 'proper' gender, a gender proper to one sex rather than another, which is in some sense that sex's cultural property. Where that notion of the 'proper' operates, it is always and only *im*properly installed as the effect of a compulsory system" ("Imitation and Gender Insubordination," in *Inside Out: Lesbian Theories, Gay Theories,* ed. Diana Fuss [New York: Routledge, 1991], 21). My reading of Cleland is indebted to Butler.

10. See William Epstein, *John Cleland: Images of a Life* (New York: Columbia University Press, 1974), 120–27.

11. Epstein, *John Cleland*, 121.

12. *Memoirs of a Coxcomb* (1751; reprinted as part of the series *The Flowering of the Novel: Representative Mid-Eighteenth Century Fiction, 1740–1775,* New York: Garland, 1974). All citations are from this edition.

13. After watching Polly and her Genoese lover have intercourse, Fanny becomes impatient with Phoebe's attentions and begins to pine "for more solid food, and promis'd tacitly to myself that I would not be put off much longer with this foolery from woman to woman" (34).

14. See *Memoirs of a Coxcomb*, 7.

15. *Pace* Kopelson.

16. Leo Braudy points out that *Memoirs of a Woman of Pleasure* exploits the traits of sentimentalism that this episode between Fanny and Charles exemplifies: "Many of the themes I have found in *Fanny Hill* sound much like those usually associated with sentimentalism: the truth of feelings and instincts, the natural as the basic part of human nature, the superiority of nature to art, the inadequacy of language, and social egalitarianism" ("*Fanny Hill* and Materialism," *Eighteenth-Century Studies* 4 [1970]: 39).

17. Julia Epstein aptly describes "Fanny's Richardsonian 'writing to

the moment' skills" as a technique by which "absolute presence takes over, then explodes" ("Fanny's Fanny," 138).

18. Fanny's breasts are distinguished by "their pride, whiteness, fashion, pleasing resistance to the touch" (39) so as to concatenate whiteness with beauty and youth—that is, with Charles.

19. Fanny comments insistently on Charles' "all-perfect manly beauty," on the "strength of manhood" veiled by his youthful body, and on the "manly proportions" of his chest (44) without ever admiring him for his "manly" penis, presumably because that would be ontologically redundant.

20. The first she sees belongs to Mrs. Brown's horse-grenadier (25).

21. "What Fanny Felt: The Pain of Compliance in *Memoirs of a Woman of Pleasure*," *Studies in the Novel* 19 (1987): 290.

22. Braudy apparently accepts as unproblematic the referential hierarchy at work in this passage: "Penises are compared to ivory columns and breasts to marble so that their actual superiority to these things of art may be clear" ("*Fanny Hill* and Materialism," 39).

23. Sabor writes in his introduction to *Memoirs of a Woman of Pleasure* that "there are over fifty metaphorical variations for the penis" (xix).

24. Braudy highlights this similarity between the two types of penile rhetoric when he asserts that "the language of mechanism and the invocation of nature are therefore total complements in *Fanny Hill*, although later pornographic works, in which great machines penetrate mossy grots, have undoubtedly lost this kind of understanding" ("*Fanny Hill* and Materialism," 37–38).

25. Flynn cites this passage as evidence that Cleland's phallocentric fantasy is based on the fear of phallic insensibility: "Central to this fantasy is not phallocentric power, but the fear rendered ironic through hyperbole that the phallus lacks the power to be felt" ("What Fanny Felt," 292). Such fear is, I think, a special case of the anxiety that there may be no necessary relationship between male and female bodies. Both phallic inadequacy and phallic displacement indicate a breakdown in the logic of natural correspondence.

26. This potential disintegration of sexual difference is what distinguishes Cleland's concept of the fetish from Freud's. For Freud, the fetishistic dis-

placement of libidinal impulses from female genitalia onto "inappropriate" objects confirms male identity, albeit in a disabled form: "Furthermore, an aversion which is never absent in any fetishist, to the real female genitals remains a *stigma indelibile* of the repression that has taken place. We can now see what the fetish achieves and what it is that maintains it. It remains a token of triumph over the threat of castration and a protection from it. It also saves the fetishist from becoming a homosexual, by endowing women with the characteristic that makes them tolerable as sexual objects." Castration anxiety thus guarantees the coherence of male identity: "Probably no male human being is spared the fright of castration at the sight of a female genital" ("Fetishism," trans. Joan Riviere, in *The Future of an Illusion, Civilization and Its Discontents, and Other Works*, ed. James Strachey, vol. 21 of *The Standard Edition of the Complete Psychological Works of Sigmund Freud* [London: Hogarth Press, 1961], 154). Since the fetish is a substitute for the maternal phallus, Freud might seem to complicate the referentiality of sexual difference in a way Cleland does not, but both men actually represent fetishized objects as marks of this difference. For Freud, fetishes insist on the "lack" and "difference" of the female body, while for Cleland, they signify a detour from purposive heterosexual intercourse that nevertheless indicates the natural outcome of sexually differentiated desires.

27. Paradoxically, Fanny suggests that the "exotic," even erotic content of this scene goes on in exactly the same way that nothing would be going on if the old man were a "she" like Fanny herself. She thus conjures up an image of lesbian sexuality in the very act of dismissing such sexuality.

28. As Donald Mengay has noted: "In the sodomitical passage the reader finds the rhetoric of penetration strikingly similar to that of Fanny's heterosexual language. Having forgotten her own experience with Charles, in which her initial 'narrowness' adjusted *for the time* to his penis size, all of a sudden Fanny again ponders the mechanics of insertion" ("The Sodomitical Muse: *Fanny Hill* and the Rhetoric of Crossdressing," in *Homosexuality in Renaissance and Enlightenment England*, ed. Summers, 193).

29. Lee Edelman theorizes the contradiction informing Mrs. Cole's remarks when he writes, "yet if the cultural enterprise of reading homosexuality would affirm that the homosexual is distinctively and *legibly*

marked, it must also recognize that those markings have been, can be, or can pass as, unremarked and unremarkable" ("Homographesis," *Yale Journal of Criticism* 3 [1989]: 192).

30. As Flynn does when she calls Cleland's conclusion an "ironically moralistic tail-piece" ("What Fanny Felt," 293), or as Miller does when she hypothesizes that "perhaps the miraculous feminization which attends the man who speaks the suffering of absence resembles inversion too closely in a century preoccupied with the grammar of sexual identity to be spoken with comfort even in fiction" ("'I's in Drag," 57).

Bibliography

Armstrong, Nancy. *Desire and Domestic Fiction*. Oxford: Oxford University Press, 1987.

Backsheider, Paula. "'I Died for Love': Esteem in Eighteenth-Century Novels by Women." In *Fetter'd or Free? British Women Novelists, 1670–1815*, ed. Mary Anne Schofield and Cecilia Macheski, 152–68. Athens: Ohio University Press, 1986.

Ballaster, Ros. *Seductive Forms: Women's Amatory Fiction from 1684 to 1740*. Oxford: Clarendon Press, 1992.

Bogel, F. V. *Acts of Knowledge: Pope's Later Poems*. Lewisburg, Pa.: Bucknell University Press, 1981.

Boyce, Benjamin. *The Character-Sketches in Pope's Poems*. Durham, N.C.: Duke University Press, 1962.

———. *The Theophrastan Character in England to 1642*. Cambridge: Harvard University Press, 1947.

Braudy, Leo. "*Fanny Hill* and Materialism." *Eighteenth-Century Studies* 4 (1970): 21–40.

Brennan, Teresa. Introduction to *Between Feminism and Psycho-analysis*. Ed. Teresa Brennan. London: Routledge, 1989.

Brooks-Davies, Douglas. "The Mythology of Love: Veneran (and related)

Iconography in Pope, Fielding, Cleland, and Sterne." In *Sexuality in Eighteenth-Century Britain*, ed. Paul-Gabriel Boucé. Manchester: Manchester University Press, 1982.

Brown, Laura. *Alexander Pope*. Oxford: Basil Blackwell, 1985.

————. *Ends of Empire: Women and Ideology in Early Eighteenth-Century English Literature*. Ithaca, N.Y.: Cornell University Press, 1993.

Brown, Norman O. *Life Against Death: The Psychoanalytic Meaning of History*. Middletown, Conn.: Wesleyan University Press, 1985.

Burg, B. R. "Ho Hum, Another Work of the Devil: Buggery and Sodomy in Early Stuart England." In *Historical Perspectives on Homosexuality*, ed. Salvatore J. Licata and Robert Petersen, 69–78. New York: Haworth Press, 1981.

Butler, Judith. "Imitation and Gender Insubordination." In *Inside Out: Lesbian Theories, Gay Theories*, ed. Diana Fuss, 13–31. New York: Routledge, 1991.

Campbell, Jill. "'When Men Women Turn': Gender Reversals in Fielding's Plays." In *The New Eighteenth Century*, ed. Felicity Nussbaum and Laura Brown, 62–83. New York: Methuen, 1987.

————. "Politics and Sexuality in Portraits of John, Lord Hervey." *Word & Image* 6 (1990): 281–97.

Carr, Richard [?]. *Dr. Carr's Medicinal Epistles upon Several Occasions*. Trans. John Quincy. London: William Newton and J. Phillips, 1714.

Cleland, John. *Memoirs of a Coxcomb*. New York: Garland, 1974.

————. *Memoirs of a Woman of Pleasure*. Ed. Peter Sabor. Oxford: Oxford University Press, 1985.

Cohen, Ed. "Legislating the Norm: From Sodomy to Gross Indecency." In *Displacing Homophobia: Gay Male Perspectives in Literature and Culture*, ed. Ronald R. Butters, John M. Clum, and Michael Moon, 169–205. Durham, N.C.: Duke University Press, 1989.

Congreve, William. Preface to *Incognita*. Reprinted in *Oroonoko, or The Royal Slave*, ed. Lore Metzger. New York: Norton, 1973.

Culler, Jonathan. *The Pursuit of Signs: Semiotics, Literature, Deconstruction*. Ithaca, N.Y.: Cornell University Press, 1981.

————. *Structuralist Poetics*. London: Routledge and Kegan Paul, 1975.

Dollimore, Jonathan. *Sexual Dissidence: Augustine to Wilde, Freud to Foucault*. Oxford: Clarendon Press, 1991.

Edelman, Lee. "Homographesis." *The Yale Journal of Criticism* 3 (1989): 189–207.

Edwards, Thomas. *This Dark Estate: A Reading of Pope*. Berkeley: University of California Press, 1963.

Ehrenpreis, Irvin. *Dean Swift*. Vol. 3 of *Swift: The Man, His Works, and the Age*. Cambridge: Harvard University Press, 1983.

England, A. B. *Energy and Order in the Poetry of Swift*. Lewisburg, Pa.: Bucknell University Press, 1980.

Epstein, Julia. "Either/Or—Neither/Both: Sexual Ambiguity and the Ideology of Gender." *Genders* 7 (1990): 99–142.

———. "Fanny's Fanny: Epistolarity, Eroticism, and the Transsexual Text." In *Writing the Female Voice: Essays on Epistolary Literature*, ed. Elizabeth Goldsmith, 135–53. Boston: Northeastern University Press, 1989.

Epstein, William. *John Cleland: Images of a Life*. New York: Columbia University Press, 1974.

Flynn, Carol H. *The Body in Swift and Defoe*. Cambridge: Cambridge University Press, 1990.

———. "What Fanny Felt: The Pain of Compliance in *Memoirs of a Woman of Pleasure*." *Studies in the Novel* 19 (1987): 284–95.

Freud, Sigmund. "Fetishism." Trans. Joan Riviere. In *The Future of an Illusion, Civilization and its Discontents, and Other Works*, vol. 21 of *The Standard Edition of the Complete Psychological Works of Sigmund Freud*, ed. James Strachey, 152–57. London: Hogarth Press, 1961.

Gilman, Sander. *Disease and Representation: Images of Illness from Madness to AIDS*. Ithaca, N.Y.: Cornell University Press, 1988.

Greene, Donald. "On Swift's 'Scatological' Poems." In *Essential Articles for the Study of Jonathan Swift's Poetry*, ed. David M. Vieth, 219–34. Hamden, Conn.: Shoestring Press, 1984.

Haywood, Eliza Fowler. *Philidore and Placentia, or L'Amour trop Delicat*. Reprinted in *Four Before Richardson: Selected English Novels, 1720–*

1727, ed. William H. McBurney. Lincoln: University of Nebraska Press, 1963.

Hyde, H. Montgomery. *The Love that Dared not Speak Its Name: A Candid History of Homosexuality in Britain.* Boston: Little, Brown, 1970.

Kopelson, Kevin. "Seeing Sodomy: *Fanny Hill*'s Blinding Vision." In *Homosexuality in Renaissance and Enlightenment England,* ed. Claude Summers, 173–83. New York: Harrington Park Press, 1992.

Laqueur, Thomas. *Making Sex: Body and Gender from the Greeks to Freud.* Cambridge: Harvard University Press, 1990.

———. "Orgasm, Generation, and the Politics of Reproductive Biology." *Representations* 14 (1986): 1–41.

Lee, Jae Num. *Swift and Scatological Satire.* Albuquerque: University of New Mexico Press, 1971.

Leranbaum, Miriam. *Alexander Pope's "Opus Magnum."* Oxford: Clarendon Press, 1977.

McFarlane, Cameron. *The Sodomite in Fiction and Satire, 1660–1750.* New York: Columbia University Press, 1997.

McIntosh, Mary. "The Homosexual Role." In *The Making of the Modern Homosexual,* ed. Kenneth Plummer, 30–49. London: Hutchinson, 1981.

McKeon, Michael. *The Origins of the English Novel, 1600–1740.* Baltimore: Johns Hopkins University Press, 1987.

Mengay, Donald. "The Sodomitical Muse: *Fanny Hill* and the Rhetoric of Crossdressing." In *Homosexuality in Renaissance and Enlightenment England,* ed. Claude Summers, 185–98. New York: Harrington Park Press, 1992.

Miller, Nancy. "'I's in Drag: The Sex of Recollection." *The Eighteenth Century: Theory and Interpretation.* 22 (1981): 47–57.

Morris, David B. *Alexander Pope: The Genius of Sense.* Cambridge: Harvard University Press, 1984.

Nussbaum, Felicity. *The Brink of All We Hate: English Satires on Women, 1660–1750.* Lexington: University Press of Kentucky, 1984.

———. "Pope's 'To a Lady' and the Eighteenth-Century Woman." *Philological Quarterly* 54 (1975): 444–56.

Onania; or the Heinous Sin of Self-Pollution. Reprint. New York: Garland, 1986.

Pollak, Ellen. *The Poetics of Sexual Myth: Gender and Ideology in the Verse of Swift and Pope.* Chicago: University of Chicago Press, 1985.

Pope, Alexander. *The Poems of Alexander Pope.* Ed. John Butt. New Haven: Yale University Press, 1963.

————. *Epistles to Several Persons.* Vol. 3 of *The Twickenham Edition of the Poems of Alexander Pope.* Ed. F. W. Bateson. New Haven: Yale University Press, 1951.

Richetti, John J. *Popular Fiction before Richardson: Narrative Patterns, 1700–1739.* Oxford: Clarendon Press, 1969.

Rousseau, G. S. "The Pursuit of Homosexuality in the Eighteenth Century: 'Utterly Confused Category' and/or Rich Repository?" In *'Tis Nature's Fault: Unauthorized Sexuality during the Enlightenment,* ed. Robert Maccubbin, 132–68. Cambridge: Cambridge University Press, 1985.

Schofield, Mary Anne. *Eliza Haywood.* Boston: Twayne, 1985.

————. *Quiet Rebellion: The Fictional Heroines of Eliza Fowler Haywood.* Washington, D.C.: University Press of America, 1982.

Sedgwick, Eve K. *Between Men: English Literature and Male Homo-social Desire.* New York: Columbia University Press, 1985.

————. *Epistemology of the Closet.* Berkeley: University of California Press, 1990.

Spacks, Patricia M. *An Argument of Images: The Poetry of Alexander Pope.* Cambridge: Harvard University Press, 1971.

Spencer, Jane. *The Rise of the Woman Novelist: From Aphra Behn to Jane Austen.* Oxford: Basil Blackwell, 1986.

Snitow, Ann Barr. "Mass Market Romance: Pornography for Women is Different." In *Powers of Desire: The Politics of Sexuality,* ed. Ann Barr Snitow, Christine Stansell, and Sharon Thompson, 245–63. New York: Monthly Review Press, 1983.

Straub, Kristina. "Men from Boys: Cibber, Pope, and the Schoolboy." *The Eighteenth Century: Theory and Interpretation* 3 (1991): 219–39.

Swift, Jonathan. *Jonathan Swift: The Complete Poems.* Ed. Pat Rogers. New Haven: Yale University Press, 1983.

———. *The Writings of Jonathan Swift.* Ed. Robert A. Greenberg and William Bowman Piper. New York: Norton, 1973.

Spitz, René A. "Authority and Masturbation: Some Remarks on a Bibliographical Investigation." *The Yearbook of Psycho-analysis* 9 (1953): 113–45.

Stone, Lawrence. *The Crisis of the Aristocracy, 1558–1641.* Oxford: Clarendon Press, 1965.

———. *The Family, Sex and Marriage in England, 1500–1800.* New York: Harper & Row, 1979.

Trumbach, Randolph. "The Birth of the Queen." In *Hidden from History: Reclaiming the Gay and Lesbian Past*, ed. Martin Duberman, Martha Vicinus, and George Chauncey Jr., 129–40. New York: New American Library, 1989.

———. "Sodomitical Assaults, Gender Role, and Sexual Development in Eighteenth-Century London." In *The Pursuit of Sodomy: Male Homosexuality in Renaissance and Enlightenment Europe*, ed. Kent Gerard and Gert Hekma, 407–29. New York: Harrington Park Press, 1989.

———. "Sodomitical Subcultures, Sodomitical Roles, and the Gender Revolution of the Eighteenth Century: The Recent Historiography." In *'Tis Nature's Fault: Unauthorized Sexuality during the Enlightenment*, ed. Robert Maccubbin, 109–21. Cambridge: Cambridge University Press, 1985.

———, ed. "The Tryal and Condemnation of Mervin, Lord Audley of Castlehaven, at Westminster. April the 5th 1631." In *Sodomy Trials: Seven Documents*, 1–31. New York: Garland, 1986.

Wagner, Peter. "The Veil of Medicine and Morality: Some Pornographic Aspects of the *Onania*." *British Journal for Eighteenth Century Studies* 2 (1983): 179–84.

Warburton, William. *The Works of Alexander Pope Esq. In Nine Volumes Complete. . . . Together with the Commentary and Notes of*

Mr. Warburton. 1751. Reprinted in *Pope: The Critical Heritage*, ed. John Barnard, 361–65. London: Routledge and Kegan Paul, 1973.

Wyrick, Deborah Baker. *Jonathan Swift and the Vested Word*. Chapel Hill: University of North Carolina Press, 1988.

Index